TO SAVE A LIFE

AMERSFOORT
STOMPERT
Leusden
Amersveld
Stoutenburg
Achttienhoven
Den Dolder
Soesterberg
Maarsen
Zuilen
Vecht
Bilthoven
De Bilt
Huis ter Heide
Haarzuilen
De Haar
Houten
PYRAMID
Scherpe
UTRECHT
Zeist
Austerlitz
Woudenberg
Karmelen
Veldhuizen
Oude Rijn
Oudenrijn
Bunnik
Rijzenburg
Maarn
Doorn
DARTHUIZERBERG
Montfoort
Jutfaas
Vechten
Odijk
Driebergen
Snellerwaard
IJselstein
Houten
Werkhoven
Kromme
Goeier Wetering
AMERO
Benschop
Vreeswijk
Waal
Amsterdam
Neerlangbroek
Leersum
ERWAARD
Schalkwijk
Koten
Amerongen
Ameroogen
Els
Loopik
Vianen
Tul
Wijk bij Duurstede
Jaarsveld
Hagestein
Everdingen
Ameide
Leksmond
VIJFHEEREN
Heikop
Kuilenburg
Beusichem
Zoelmond
Maurik
Lienden
Meerkerk
Schoonewoerd
Leerbroek
NEDERBETUWE
Zoelen
Echteld
Noordeloos
LANDEN
Nieuwland
Leerdam
Buren
Buurmalsen
Drumpt
Tiel
Hoogmaar
Linge
Asperen
Beesd
Deil
Tricht
Geldermalsen
Wamel
Hoogbloklands
Kedichem
Heukelom
Arkel
Wadenooien
Est
Ophemert
MAAS EN
luinen
Dreumel
TIELERWAARD
Vuren
Waardenburg
Opijnen
Varik
Alfen
Gorkum
Herwijnen
Haaften
waarden
Brakel
Zuilichem
Gameren
Zaltbommel
Rossum
Andries
LAND VAN
Poederooien
Veen
Kerkwijk
Kerkdriel
Maren
ALTENA
Almkerk
Giesen
Andel
BOMMELERWAARD
Ammersooien
Empel
Geffen
Nieuwedijk
Dussen
LAND
Wijk
Nederhemert
Hedel
Hertogswetering
Voorn
Beersche
Os
Meeuwen
Aalburg
Genderen
Eten
Drongelen
Heusden
Herpt
Engelen
Rosmalen
Nuland
Bergsch
VAN
Kapelle
Elshout
Vlijmen
's HERTOGENBOSCH
Berlikum
Waspik
Waalwijk
Drunen
Nieuwkuik
Langstraat
Sprang
Vucht
Dungen
Reeswijk
Vrijhoeve Kapelle
Gravenmoer
Kaatsheuvel
Afwateringskanaal
Kromvoort

To Save a Life
Memoirs of a Dutch Resistance Courier

by
ELSA CASPERS

Edited by JILL SUTCLIFFE

Foreword by General Sir John Hackett

A DEIRDRE McDONALD BOOK
London

First published in 1995
by Deirdre McDonald Books
128 Lower Richmond Road
London SW15 1LN
Copyright © Elsa Caspers 1995

ISBN 1 898094 10 1

Designed by Mick Keates
Typeset by Concise Artisans
Printed and bound in Great Britain by Redwood Books

The publishers gratefully acknowledge A. de Visser
of Gardata for supplying film for the illustrations

Contents

To my sister Ank
who took over my tasks
as the eldest child in our family

Author's note:

This book does not pretend to give a full account of the Dutch Resistance. It tells you some stories about the members of the Resistance in the area called 'the Utrecht chain of hills'.

After I had written two Dutch books on this subject, I was asked by some of my British friends to write something in English. In doing this I was very fortunate in obtaining the help of Jill Sutcliffe, who not only edited the book, but made me write about myself. She so skilfully kept asking for more details that I remembered things that I had long ago pushed away in my subconscious. I was used to writing local history which was quite different from writing a personal account. Jill instinctively knew what questions to ask to improve the story I had written. I am very grateful to her for making this book so much more readable than it would have been without her help.

However hard one tries it is never possible to reproduce in words exactly how life was lived in those days. The ever-present danger, tension and possibility of betrayal, cannot be expressed in words. One can only try to show some of the atmosphere of life at that time. In writing this book, I hope that my readers will understand something of the deeper motives that made people become members of the Resistance. Although there were many different reasons for joining, there was one common denominator: not being able to endure the restriction of freedom and the infringement of the integrity of our fellow men.

Elsa Caspers

Foreword by General Sir John Hackett

I approach the task of contributing a foreword to the book by Elsa Caspers, *To Save a Life*, with diffidence. My own life, or at least fifty years of it, I owe to a surgical miracle performed by a Jewish officer in the British Royal Army Medical Corps, who removed from my lower intestine a shell splinter which had inflicted ten perforations and two sections. This was done against the advice of the surgeon of the German Wehrmacht who, in St Elizabeth's Hospital in Arnhem, which was then under German control, advised that the principle of triage then being followed left no doubt that I should be allowed to die, rather than to have valuable time and equipment spent in trying to save what was clearly a doomed casualty.

Lipmann Kessel, the man who performed this surgical miracle, has since died and, to meet his own known wishes, was buried in Holland. He was one of the very many among us, in the British First Airborne Division, who came to admire, respect and love the Dutch and had remained their devoted friend. Lippy Kessel could not be buried in the war cemetery near Oosterbeek for his death was not directly attributable to action on the battlefield. A grave plot in the civilian cemetery contiguous to the war cemetery was found for him and there he rests in peace. It was he who saved my life. It was preserved thereafter by the action of brave and devoted Dutch men and women who hid, nursed, cherished, fed, clothed and protected this wounded British officer for the next four and a half months, with great danger to themselves, until it was possible for me to make my exit from Nazi-occupied Holland in the hunger-winter that followed the battle. The house in which I was looked after by three Dutch ladies – two spinsters and one widow with her grown-up son and daughter – was at 5 Torenstaat in Ede, fifty metres away from the house next door which was a German military police billet. In the event it was the work of the son in this household that brought me out of all those dangers and set me on the way back to my own home in Britain and to freedom.

The young man in question (referred to in this book as Hans van Renkum) was known to me as Johan (or, in my own form, John) Snoek, and he and his unmarried sister Mary, who did most of the active nursing in that household (now a retired welfare officer and missionary) remain very close friends with my own family.

Back in England in 1945/6, with everything still sharp and fresh in my mind, I wrote down an account of the time I was looked after with such Christian courage and compiled a manuscript under the not surprising title of *I Was a Stranger*. This was then put away for thirty years before publication in Britain by Chatto & Windus in 1978.

The reason for this somewhat lengthy explanation of how I come to be written about in this remarkable book by Elsa Caspers is simply a need to explain why I figure in its pages at all. The reason why I am anxious to do what I can to meet the wishes of the author, whom I promised a foreword to the English version of her book, is that I have nowhere found a more telling, well-informed, beautifully presented description of the life lived in Holland during the worst period of Nazi dominance.

I have been largely instrumental in raising funds and guiding action for the erection of a memorial in the grounds of the Hartenstein Airborne Museum in Oosterbeek, offering a tribute to the citizens of Gelderland who, in the dark days, took so many of us into their homes and found their own place in all our hearts. I was able to unveil this memorial, with its inscription, in Hartenstein Park on 14 September 1994, at the outset of the ceremonies commemorating the 50th Anniversary of the battle for the Arnhem bridge, which we were ordered to take and hold for two days until relieved by the British Second Army. In the event we fought for nine days without relief and with heavy casualties, until a total exhaustion of ammunition together with food and water and other necessities destroyed what remained of the airborne defenders at the Arnhem bridge. The remainder of the defence (or as much of it as could be got out) crossed the Lower Rhine to rejoin the allies. Over ten thousand airborne men were put in by parachute or glider and of them nearly seven thousand never came out, with some two thousand dead and the rest captured. In the Fourth Parachute Brigade, which I commanded until being wounded for the second time (on this occasion very seriously) on 25 September, two thousand three hundred parachutists jumped in with me on 18 September and only a few more than two hundred came out. This is not the place to explore the combination of misjudgement, planning mistakes, misfortunes, poor communications, bad weather and other factors which combined to make Operation 'Market Garden' a failure. After sixteen abortive operational plans and often last-minute cancellations, this magnificent division, the British First Airborne, had to be got into action before it began to go downhill. Going in on the second lift on 18 September, when the main part of the division had landed the day before, we found a situation with surprise (the most effective weapon of airborne troops) totally dissipated and German opposition, with unexpected armour, already formed up against us. We were in no uncertainty about what we were in for and, as one surviving old airborne recently expressed a view held by so many, 'we knew we were doomed before we set out'. This did nothing whatsoever to diminish the enthusiasm and even the zest with which a splendid body of highly trained and motivated fighting men went in to what could only be regarded as a hopeless battle.

The resolution, the courage, the fortitude and the Christian charity of the Dutch civilians, who had every reason to resent what we did to them, has always, considerably to our surprise, left no hostility or bitterness towards us who caused it. Instead we remain, on our side, full of gratitude for what they did for us and for the forgiveness we enjoy for what we airbornes did to our Dutch friends.

I shall never forget what Elsa Caspers did for me and for others in helping our escape and rejoice that my family have forged such a strong bond of friendship with her and with others who helped me to get out of occupied Holland and back to my own home. I have long been registered, in the brilliantly forged document which attests my origin, as Johan van Dalen, born in Renkum on 5 November 1910, now a citizen of Ede.

It was an unforgettable experience to be for so long a wounded British fugitive in hiding and a participant in a remarkable series of adventures as well as their principal beneficiary; and I shall always be grateful to Elsa Caspers for putting together this exact and moving book, and for the opportunity to make a contribution to it. I am confident that *To Save a Life* will meet the recognition it deserves.

Prologue

The men and women I knew in the Dutch Resistance during the Second World War did not, as far as I know, make a conscious decision to 'join' it. Usually what happened was that someone you knew and trusted asked you to undertake some specific task, such as carrying documents from one place to another, hiding someone in your house, giving food or money, and so on. After that you became committed to the cause and never looked back.

It was a strange kind of job: there was no formal interview for it, no psychological test, no training, and no pay. And if you made a mistake, or were just unlucky, *you* could pay with your life and perhaps the lives of others too.

It helped to be young and single, as I was, for you had no dependants (though no doubt our parents and siblings worried about us). Not that all Resistance workers were young. Many were married, with families to think of, but they still put what they saw as their duty – Christian, patriotic or social – first.

How did I feel about what I was doing? Different ways on different days. I felt anger and powerlessness when a friend had been executed. The day three friends died (Frans, Ted and Bob, see chapter 7) we were all devastated but the more determined to go on fighting. I felt satisfaction and elation when a job was well done, and I felt despair at moments when I did not know where to go because all the safe addresses seemed to have been rumbled, and at such times I experienced such complete loneliness as I have never known since. There were many uncertainties: sometimes I slept every night of the week in a different bed and not always in very pleasant circumstances. Once, things were going so badly that I had only one safe address to go to, in Veenendaal, a town on the other side of the hills, to the east of Driebergen. It was in a terrible slum but with the kindest people imaginable. They did not even have a WC in those days – just a barrel in a shed, which was emptied twice a week. We slept five in one double bed that night. If one of us turned in our sleep, everyone woke up. Nevertheless there was a tremendous feeling of camaraderie, and we were thankful to be safe for the time being at least. Sometimes we were terribly afraid. When friends had been arrested, we did not know how much the Germans knew. Although we all thought we would never tell the Germans anything, who knows what anyone might have said under intense pressure or even torture? After an arrest it required real courage to ring someone's doorbell while you crossed your fingers that it wouldn't be a German soldier who opened the door to you.

Everything was very informal. We knew each other only by a Christian name, and that was usually an assumed one. In Dutch there is a familiar and polite form of address, as with the French *tu* and *vous*. We used only the familiar form. You rarely knew a person's profession or trade – the less you knew, the safer it was. My friends in the Resistance were from all walks of life. In normal circumstances many of us would never have met, but because of the Resistance comradeship we had a really classless society, and that was marvellous. Friendships we made then have lasted for life.

Although at the start of the occupation I still lived at home, being only fifteen years old, within three years I had become involved with the Resistance and had to go and live elsewhere. I missed my parents and my family. In the last year I saw them perhaps once every two months or so.

I still feel guilty because I was not at home to help with obtaining food and fuel, both of which became extremely scarce as time went on. My brother was away at boarding school in Nijmegen from 1941, when he was fifteen, until the battle of Arnhem started and the boys were sent home. He had to become a 'diver' then (see page 15) because the Germans were calling up all men aged between seventeen and fifty to go and work in Germany. Since he was still registered as living in Nijmegen, and the neighbours did not know he had returned to Driebergen, he was able to hide at home, but he could never go out, which was very frustrating, and he could not help obtain food or fuel. Instead, my underfed fourteen-year-old sister Ank had to go and hack down small pine trees in the forest and bring the wood home, a job far too heavy for a young girl.

I still feel excluded now whenever my sister talks about the 'Hunger-winter' and I can't join in. I miss having no shared memories about the most traumatic time of our lives. For example, when my father died in 1992 and we were clearing the house, a small packing case was brought out of the cellar. It was the 'cart' – minus the wheels – that my sister had always used to bring wood from the forest. She burst into tears at seeing it again for the first time in almost fifty years. I felt so helpless, not even knowing what memories that cart had brought back to her.

She told me then how my father had mounted the packing case, which measured about one metre long and half a metre wide (3ft 3in × 1ft 7in), on two bicycle wheels without tyres. Because the wheels were large the axle was high off the ground and it was difficult to keep a full cart balanced. Many times it would tip over in the snow (there was a lot of snow in December 1944 and the first two months of 1945), the lid would fly open and the wood would fall out. Ank would then have to reload it. It would have been simple to tie the lid on with string but that was unobtainable.

One day when she was in the woods and had started on a tree, the air-raid siren went, but of course she was too far from home to return. She saw four British planes fly over very low on their way to attack the railway line, which the RAF did regularly since it was an important line for the Germans. Almost immediately one plane returned, as it had been hit by flak. To gain height the pilot had to jettison his bombs. He must have seen the large coniferous forest and thought it was the safest place to drop his load. The first bomb fell near Maarn, about 3 km (1½ miles) away. Then, in quick succession, four more were dropped while the plane flew toward Driebergen. As Ank threw herself to the ground she saw out of the corner of her eye a huge column of sand go up, and when she stood up again she found a large splinter measuring 15 cm by 6 cm (6in × 2¼in) lying within a metre of her, and other pieces of metal were near by. When everything was quiet again, it occurred to her that the bombs might have uprooted some of the trees and that this would save her a lot of work. This proved to be the case, so she cut them up with her small axe and obtained enough wood for a really full load. She always took a folding ruler with her so that she could cut the wood to fit inside the packing case. At last she went home, well satisfied with what she had collected and took with her the splinters to show her mother.

When Ank arrived home, my mother was at the garden gate, being comforted by the vicar. The all-clear had sounded ages ago and Ank had not returned. It was now hours past her usual time. The house had shuddered a bit when the bombs fell, though the windows had remained intact – but Mother was terribly worried about Ank. When she saw the bomb splinters she almost collapsed with shock.

Next day Ank went woodcutting again. She was just starting on a tree when a plane came over. It was then that she suddenly suffered delayed shock from the previous day. She ran into the forest, dropping her axe and leaving her cart. She became completely lost – and the forest stretched all the way to Maarn. At last she calmed down and managed to find her way back. By a stroke of luck she even found her axe (a most precious possession in those days), and the cart was still there. Without the wood Ank brought home it would have been impossible for Mother to cook and keep the house warm.

My parents themselves supported the Resistance from the start, long before I was old enough to take an active part. Our house was a safe address throughout the war, and my mother had a girl courier staying overnight every week. Once, when my mother was changing the sheets on the bed of one young diver we had with us, she found a gun under his pillow. After that she made him change his own sheets, as she did not want to handle weapons. Secret meetings took place at our house too. Wilma, my youngest sister, then went out in the street to play with her marbles and to keep a look out. Apart from that, we were an emergency address in case a Jewish person had to move suddenly. I remember one such occasion when in one household where Jewish divers were hiding the host had fallen in love with a Jewish girl. His wife had hit the roof. All the Jewish people in their house had to leave immediately. My mother took one of them in. They never stayed long, though, as our house had to be kept safe for the general purposes of the Resistance.

My parents knew I was in the Resistance but they never knew what I was doing or with whom I worked. I doubt if they could have found me quickly in an emergency. At one stage the Germans started questioning children hoping to obtain information that way. As a precaution my parents then sent Wilma, who was nine years old, away to stay with friends. I felt very sorry for Wilma, she must have missed 'home' so much. They also hid all the family photographs that had me on them in a neighbour's clock in case the Gestapo came to search our house.

The story I shall tell in the following chapters is about the activities of the Resistance in some of the towns and villages in the chain of hills south-east of Utrecht, and the part I played in it. I hope also to give you some idea of what conditions were like for the civilian population in an occupied country. Nowadays I visit schools in the Netherlands to tell the children about this time in their history, so that they may learn from it. The price of liberty is eternal vigilance.

Caspers family photograph, 1949
From left to right: Ank, Wilma, Father, Ruud, Mother, Author

1

The Occupation Begins

Introduction

While Nazism gathered strength in the 1930s and Hitler pursued his territorial ambitions and racist policies, first in Austria and then in Czechoslovakia, the citizens of the other European nations – that is the non-politically active majority of 'ordinary' people – went on with their daily lives. They worked, if they had a job, for the 1930s were years of economic depression and unemployment in Europe generally, much as we have known it again in recent times. They brought up their families; and they enjoyed what leisure time they had.

In the Netherlands my family, the Caspers, lived in Driebergen, which in those days was a small town of about 10,000 people. Driebergen, as its name 'Three hills' suggests, is situated on the edge of the chain of hills which curls round to the east of Utrecht and reaches the Rhine at Rhenen. The area is full of forests and heathland.

The family consisted of my father Willem, my mother Fenna, me, my younger brother and two younger sisters. Since the war I have been called Elsa, the name I was usually (though not always) known by in the Dutch Resistance. I was born in 1924. My brother, Ruud, was born in 1926, and my sisters, Ank and Wilma, were born in 1930 and 1935 respectively.

My father was appointed headmaster of the local Protestant school in Driebergen in 1921. My mother had also been a teacher but in those days women were not allowed to continue to teach once they were married, so she became a housewife and mother, running the house with the help of a maid, which was the accepted norm for a professional household at that time. Housekeeping was much more arduous and complicated then, as there were few of the labour-saving devices we take for granted today. On the other hand there was

1

not much shopping to be done because the milkman and the baker delivered daily and the grocer and the butcher called twice a week.

The school for which my father was responsible had 400 pupils, a large number then, aged between six and fourteen, the years for which schooling was compulsory. Everyone walked to school. Some children from the outlying farms had an hour's walk, and they stayed at school for the lunch break to eat their sandwiches. This, supervised by a teacher, took only about a quarter of an hour, after which the children were free to play in the school playground. My brother and I would join them as soon as we had finished our meal at home.

My father was well liked and respected in the town. He understood children and never had any trouble with them. He was on many local committees and was an elder of the church. Although he died in 1992 at the age of ninety-seven, the local people still talk of him as a much-loved figure.

Local community life was peaceful and secure. There was practically no crime. People did not lock their houses during the day, and the theft of bicycles was almost unheard of. Sunday was strictly observed as a day for going to church and for resting. We would go for long walks in between two church services, and of course we were not allowed to ride a bicycle or to play in the street that day. During the week and on Saturdays, however, there were many social activities going on in Driebergen, and we all belonged to a basketball club and a gymnasium, and we sang in a choir.

My family was therefore well known in the town and surrounding area, and my father obviously had some standing and influence locally. As the eldest child, I was brought up to be a responsible member of society and to take an interest in what was going on in the world outside our home.

My family and friends felt that war was going to be inevitable one day. Unlike Chamberlain in England, we did not trust Hitler. One of our next-door neighbours was a Jewish family who had fled from Germany in 1936, so we had heard first-hand accounts of the Nazi persecution of the Jews. There was a Nazi Party in the Netherlands too, but its members were forbidden to wear a uniform and they generally kept a low profile. After Munich, however, they were emboldened and their activities became more noticeable.

Many people in the Netherlands thought we would be able to remain neutral, just as we had been in the First World War. Indeed, after the invasion of Poland in 1939, when Britain and France had declared war on Germany, according to their treaty obligations, such was our Government's faith in treaties and international law that an attempt was made (unsuccessfully) to shoot down a British aeroplane which flew over our territory. The authorities issued us all with a ration card, just in case we might need one, and we had exercises in blackouts – making sure no light could be seen from our houses during the hours of darkness – and in what to do if the air-raid sirens were sounded.

My father became a member of the Citizen Guard – the Dutch equivalent of the British Home Guard. They practised shooting with rifles, and when an air-raid exercise was on he had to go out and check that all the houses in the area were properly blacked out and that no one was out in the street. As we children knew it was just an exercise we would slip outside, hoping to be caught and be ordered sternly to go indoors. To us it was just another game.

On 10 May 1940, however, we were awakened at 5 a.m. by the heavy drone of many aircraft overhead. They were German planes. We turned on the radio and heard the announcement that we were at war. The next five days were very frightening. Air-raid alerts were so frequent as to be almost permanent. My father had to go out, with his rifle, and direct the Dutch military traffic that was rushing through our town towards the 'Grebbelinie' a line of defence near Rhenen.

Everyone was bewildered when we heard on 13 May that our beloved Queen Wilhelmina had left us and gone to England. Only later did we understand that she would have been taken prisoner if she had stayed, and then we were all pleased that she was safe. Our Government had also escaped.

On 14 May the Germans sent an ultimatum, saying they would bomb Rotterdam if the Dutch army did not surrender straightaway. The German officer who brought the message added verbally that Amsterdam, The Hague, Utrecht and Haarlem would also be reduced to rubble if the ultimatum was ignored. Because the document was not clearly signed with the name and rank of the officer who issued it, the Dutch asked for this identification to be added. The German officer returned to his commander, who then wrote out and signed properly a second ultimatum which would expire at 4.20 p.m. This was handed to the Dutch at 1.15 p.m., but shortly after the expiry of the first ultimatum, German planes were heard overhead. The German commander later said he ordered Very lights to be fired to recall the planes but it was too late – a few turned and dropped their bombs elsewhere but most of them went on and bombed Rotterdam. In this act of gross brutality against a largely defenceless population, 800 civilians were killed. As our position was completely untenable, our army surrendered that evening, except for the troops in Zeeland, who fought on bravely and tenaciously for another three days.

In Driebergen, which is about 75 km (45 miles) from the frontier with Germany, we had heard the gunfire and then witnessed the withdrawal of the Dutch troops on the last day. When our army surrendered, there was a general feeling of being totally crushed. The civil authorities did their best to keep order in the general chaos.

The Dutch had not fought a war for over a hundred years, and after the surrender people were apprehensive about what would happen next. Jewish people in particular were terribly afraid that the same measures would be taken against them as had been taken in Germany, and those who had already fled from Germany and settled in the Netherlands were stricken with terror. The stories they told sounded unbelievable, but letters they had received from relatives and friends still in Germany revealed that the situation there was steadily deteriorating and was becoming actually life-threatening.

Before the war a Dutch relief committee had tried to save 10,000 Jewish children from Austria and Germany. The children were brought to the Netherlands and from Hoek van Holland the ferryboat service carried them to Harwich in groups of 150. Once there, an English relief committee had taken care of them. The target of 10,000 children had almost been reached when Nazi Germany violated Dutch neutrality.

Occupation

After two chaotic weeks, on 29 May Hitler put the Austrian Artur von Seyss-Inquart in charge of a civilian Dutch government. Seyss-Inquart made a speech at his installation in The Hague in which he promised to adhere to Dutch laws as much as possible. In the Dutch newspapers the words 'as much as possible' were not translated from the German, so a large part of the population was lulled into a false sense of security. Ever ostrich-like, people thought things might not be as bad as they had anticipated. Children were sent back to school, a programme for the rebuilding of bombed houses and other buildings was started, and life began to return to some semblance of normality. Nevertheless, the presence of German soldiers in all the towns was a constant reminder of what had happened.

The Germans imposed a curfew. At first this was from midnight until 4 a.m., but gradually it was extended, from 11 p.m., and then, after Mad Tuesday (see chapter 2), when the Germans really cracked down on us, it was from 8 p.m. until 6 a.m. Towards the very end of the war we were confined to our homes for most of the day.

The curfew meant that if we wanted to have a party – and these did continue to take place, more in the early years of the war than later, on such occasions as birthdays, engagements, and so on – we either had to be home before curfew or had to stay overnight. In some ways, for us young people, staying over was more fun than we had been allowed at pre-war parties, when of course we had to go home at a reasonable hour!

Cinemas were open, but all the films were German and the news before the main feature showed only German victories, German propaganda, Hitler inspecting troops, and so on. So none of us ever went.

We also had concerts at first, but in 1941 the Germans decreed that all musicians had to belong to a Chamber of Culture, which was a Nazi umbrella organisation. Musicians who refused to join were forbidden to perform in public. So we all stopped going.

The musicians gave concerts in private houses instead. If you had a piano you could invite friends. A pianist would play solo pieces or duets with a violinist, or there would be other chamber music, and afterwards a collection would be taken. We enjoyed these occasions very much, but, alas, they more or less came to an end when all the male musicians were called up to work in Germany.

One day a friend of my mother said, 'I have a great surprise for you. I have organised a concert and you are all invited.' We went and listened to a woman pianist who played some Chopin nocturnes. The hostess was not very musical herself and the piano had not been tuned for some time.

The hostess slipped out of the room to put the kettle on and when the last note of the opening piece sounded she said, 'Now let us all have a cup of tea.' (Some people still had some tea left then.)

The surprised pianist said, 'Oh no, the interval is not until after item five.'

So like it or not, the tea had to stew.

Sports clubs also came under a Nazi umbrella organisation, so we had to disband ours. My basketball club closed in October 1942 when our league was forbidden. Scouts and Girl Guides had been forbidden earlier, and amateur dramatics were only allowed if you belonged to a Nazi organisation.

The Protestant and Catholic churches forbade their choir members to rehearse in any building that displayed a notice saying 'Out of bounds to Jews'. The only way a church choir could put on a performance of the Messiah, for example, or a Sunday School could perform a Nativity play, was if it was made part of a service held in the church itself.

Right from the start of the occupation people did not help the Germans. When a soldier went into our local grocer's and asked for 'Marmelade' – the German word for jam – the grocer told him that those pots were not marmalade (that is, made with oranges, as in England) but something quite different. The baffled soldier left without his jam. If a German asked you the way, you sent him in the opposite direction. The ordinary soldiers of the Wehrmacht did try to be friendly, but they were not welcome in our country, and we made sure that they knew it. The only people who responded to them were members of the Dutch Nazi Party.

Less than a month after Seyss-Inquart arrived he suspended our Parliament and State Council. 'Burgemeesters' – civil servants appointed by the Home Secretary to oversee public order in Dutch towns – were allowed to stay on, but in all the towns and large villages a local Wehrmacht commander, or 'Ortskommandant', was appointed. In Driebergen we were lucky, as it turned out that the Ortskommandant had been a Lutheran pastor before he was called up into the army. He visited one of the Dutch church ministers, who agreed to talk about religious matters but not politics. This contact proved to be very useful, as sometimes the minister's appeal to the Ortskommandant on humanitarian grounds succeeded and an arrested person was allowed to go, instead of being sent on to the Gestapo.

The town of Doorn, with a population of about 5,000, and situated about 5 km (3 miles) from Driebergen, was in a different position administratively from every other town, because the ex-German Emperor, Kaiser Bill, had taken refuge there after the First World War. During the first weeks of the occupation in 1940 many high-ranking German officers presented themselves to the Kaiser while he, as usual, sat quietly in his rose garden. The Nazis were very annoyed about this, so instead of an Ortskommandant they appointed a member of the Sicherheitsdienst (SD) – the Security Service, an SS organisation – to guard the ex-emperor and to see to it that he had no more contact with army officers. After the death of the Kaiser in 1941 Doorn did have an Ortskommandant, like every other town.

The Dutch Nazi organisation NSB had a paramilitary section called 'Stormtroopers', which had been forbidden before the war. Now, the members put on their black uniforms and marched through the streets singing Nazi songs and generally behaving in a provocative manner. There was also a section called 'Youth-storm', similar to the Hitler Youth in Germany. These youngsters also wore a uniform, did a lot of sport during the weekends and were taught Nazi ideology.

In 1941 one of the Youth-storm boys in Driebergen came to school one day wearing his Nazi uniform. My father forbade him to wear it and told him to change into ordinary clothes for the afternoon class. In the evening the boy's father visited our house. He was furious with my father, and when he still did not obtain permission for his son to wear the Nazi uniform to school he threatened to take the matter further. I sat at the top of the stairs listening and hearing the Nazi's voice getting louder and louder. It was very frightening because you never knew what these men would do next. Deep in my heart, though, I was very proud of my father for taking such a stand.

Next day the chairman of the local Nazi Party, accompanied by another notorious Nazi, came to the school. When my father still would not concede the point, they threatened to complain to the SD. This turned out to be no idle threat, for a few days later he was summoned to the SD headquarters in Utrecht. I was terribly worried when he left the house. It would take him an hour to travel to Utrecht and an hour back again, apart from the interview itself, so he would be gone for a long time. I kept asking my mother if she thought he would come back. She was a very religious woman and she kept saying, 'We must trust in God. He will watch over him.'

At the interview, my father told us afterwards, the Germans said he did not have the right to forbid a boy to wear his Nazi uniform to school. My father replied that he was the headmaster of a Christian school. He could not allow a boy to wear the uniform of a Party whose ideology was against all Christian belief. They asked him to explain this further, so he said that the Nazis preferred one person to another depending on what race he or she belonged to and that this radically conflicted with the Christian faith, which teaches that before God all people are equal. In particular, discrimination against the Jewish people conflicted with everything a Christian believes in.

A lengthy record was made of this conversation and my father was asked to listen while it was read out. As he did not trust the Germans to read what was written, he told them that he would prefer to read it himself, and they agreed. At the bottom of the page were three letters. He asked what these stood for, and they told him that it was an abbreviation of three words meaning that he had listened to the reading of the statement and agreed with it. The Germans were always meticulous about administrative detail, so they changed the first letter to one meaning that he had read the statement. After all this my father was allowed to go home. It was such a relief when we saw him arriving. People were often jailed for lesser offences. The outcome of it all was that the boy never wore his uniform to school again. At least everyone in the school knew that they had to be careful what they said in front of him and his family.

The Dutch have always attached great importance to the freedom of the press, freedom of assembly, religious liberty, and so on. When Galileo wrote his *Dialogo* in 1632 it was put on the Roman Catholic Index and banned, but the Dutch printed it, in Latin of course, and from Leyden it was distributed all over the then known world. One of the first things the Germans did when they occupied the Netherlands was to take control of and muzzle the Dutch press. The result was that a number of underground papers were started up, and these contributed much to the Resistance when it became organised, and to Dutch morale generally. The first anti-German leaflet was printed and passed around on the very first day of the occupation.

The early Resistance groups concentrated on training in unarmed combat, gathering information which they hoped they would be able to find a way of sending to the Allies, and writing pamphlets against the Germans. One of the largest groups was called the Ordedienst, or OD for short. These soldiers thought that as they had sworn an oath of allegiance to the Queen they should go on fighting the enemy even after the army surrendered. They also thought that they would be needed to restore order in the country as soon as the enemy retreated, because the Dutch Government-in-exile would then still be in London. At that time everybody thought that the war would not last long. Most people, apart from the Dutch Nazis, of course, could not bear to think that the German occupation of our country would be anything but temporary.

One of the first officers in Driebergen who joined the OD was Major Du Celliée Muller, a retired officer of the Dutch East Indies Army. When the Dutch mobilised in 1939 he volunteered and was put on active service again. Much to his annoyance, his next-door neighbour was a German and a dedicated Nazi. The Dutch always celebrate birthdays and the Queen's birthday is a national holiday with many festivities: children's games; a procession in the evening with Chinese lanterns; and dances and parties all over the country. On royal birthdays flags are flown not only from official buildings but also from private houses. When, less than two months after the capitulation, Prince Bernhard's birthday occurred, on 29 June, the Dutch started hoisting their flags and putting flowers in front of the palaces, but this was soon forbidden by the Germans. When Queen Wilhelmina's birthday came, on 31 August, Du Celliée Muller put a record of the National Anthem on his gramophone, placed the gramophone on his windowsill, with the windows wide open, and hoisted the flag while the anthem was being played. His neighbour immediately called the police. A constable arrived and told the major that he was no longer allowed to do this. Du Celliée Muller said to the constable, 'Get out, or I'll shoot you. I would rather die than kowtow to those dogs.' The police, of course, were Dutch, so they took no further action, and it was not until sunset that the major lowered the flag, demonstrating his defiance of the occupying power.

At first the organisation of Resistance groups was a bit amateurish. There was not always the security there should have been. For example, sometimes lists of members were actually written down, which now with hindsight seems incredible. Being a Resistance worker, however, was a job you learnt as you went along, and inevitably mistakes – sometimes tragic ones – were made.

The Germans soon found out about the OD. The major was arrested in September 1941. His wife hired a Dutch lawyer but he was not allowed to attend the trial. All the accused were given a German lawyer, who did not help them at all. The outcome of the trial was devastating. Seventy-two men were executed and fifty-two were jailed. Most of those were sent to German concentration camps. The major went to Sachsenhausen, where he died a year later. The burgemeester received the death certificate through the Red Cross. The cause of death was given as 'pneumonia'. The burgemeester made enquiries from the Red Cross office and it turned out that all death certificates issued in Sachsenhausen concentration camp gave 'pneumonia' as the cause of death.

Trying to save the Jews
Soon after the occupation the measures against the Jews began. In January 1941 all Jews in the country had to register, and on 22 and 23 February the first round-up of Jewish men in Amsterdam took place. The Germans arrested 389 men, who were sent to Mauthausen concentration camp. Only one man survived.

The people of Amsterdam were outraged by these arrests. The whole city went on strike. Schools were closed, trams and buses stayed in their depots, and nobody went to work. The Germans were taken totally by surprise, as they had never encountered a people who took the side of the Jews. They did not apparently realise that the Dutch have always taken in people who were persecuted elsewhere. In the sixteenth century the Dutch took in Portuguese Jews, in the seventeenth century they sheltered Royalists from England, and when Hitler started persecuting the Jews in Germany and Austria they had taken those in too. It was a question of helping fellow human beings in need. Some people looked on it as their Christian duty, while others simply had humanitarian motives. After two days of the strike in Amsterdam the Germans started shooting at random at the civilian population. Several people were killed and that was the end of the protest.

The situation for Jewish people quickly worsened. They were no longer permitted to work in factories, their children were allowed to attend only Jewish schools and in more towns Jews were being rounded up. In October 1941 all civil servants had to sign a certificate stating that neither they nor their wife, husband or fiancé(e), nor any of their parents or grandparents, were Jewish. The combined Protestant Churches protested but this was to no avail. In the same months restaurants, pubs and public libraries had to display a sign saying 'No Jews allowed here'. A month later all Jewish civil servants were sacked. Students in Delft and Leyden went on strike to protest against the sacking of their Jewish professors and lecturers, whereupon the Germans closed the universities.

It was clear that the rest of us had to help the Jews. At first this help was not organised, but, nevertheless, between the end of 1941 and the beginning of 1942 many Jews managed to find a place where they could go into hiding. This was much more difficult than it sounds. Everyone from the age of fifteen upwards had to carry an identity card. This card had the owner's photograph, fingerprint and signature on it. Jewish identity cards had in addition a large letter 'J'. This idea had started in the late 1930s, when German Jews were trying to flee to Switzerland. The Swiss authorities had not liked this influx and the head of the Swiss police asked the German government to stamp Jewish passports with a 'J', which would enable the Swiss to pick out the Jews as soon as they arrived at the border. The Germans complied with the request and, later on, the documents of Jews in the occupied countries were stamped in a similar way. At any time you could be stopped in the street and asked for your identity card. This meant that Jewish people could not carry their own card if they did not want to be identified as Jews. Moreover, all Jews except children under six years of age had to wear a yellow Star of David on all their outer clothing. This made them sitting targets if they went out into the streets. Of course, as soon as a Jewish person found a hiding place those yellow stars were destroyed.

Jews were no longer allowed to live where they had always lived. They all had to go to Amsterdam, where the Germans created a Jewish ghetto. Those who lived elsewhere received a letter with the time the police would come to collect the keys to their house, after which they had to leave for Amsterdam. With this letter was a leaflet which contained the following advice:

1 Sick people: If a member of your family cannot travel because of serious illness or a disability, you will have to obtain a doctor's certificate both in German and Dutch. The certificate must state the diagnosis. Statements such as 'unable to travel' will not be accepted.

2 You are reminded that Jews in Amsterdam are allowed to live only in one of the three Jewish quarters. If necessary, the Jewish Council will try to help you to find accommodation. You are not allowed to occupy an empty house, so you will have to move in with other Jews.

3 If you have relatives still living outside the Jewish quarters, the Jewish Council will try to obtain permission for you to move in with them.

4 Don't forget to take all your papers, e.g. birth certificate, identity card, ration card, with you.

5 Take food for one day with you.

6 If you have non-Jewish servants, you will have to give them notice.

7 You will have to cancel the lease of your house.

8 Don't forget to turn off the water at the mains and to advise the gas and electricity boards of the time of your departure so that they can disconnect their services.

9 Make a list of the goods that you are leaving in the house.

10 You will have to pay all costs yourself.

Fortunately not everyone obeyed. Some were taken in by friends or friends of friends. Others were helped by total strangers. Wim Koumans, who owned a nursery for growing flowers and vegetables in Doorn, found he had become the organiser of a 'clearing-house' – as with so many members of the Resistance, by doing one anti-German act you were drawn into doing more and more. As soon as he had found an address for one or two Jews and they had been taken to their new home others would arrive at his house. After the war it turned out that he and his wife Anna had had about 200 Jewish people staying with them for longer or shorter periods. The Koumans were the parents of small children, who complained one day to their mother: 'The children at school get a new brother or sister but we only get aunties and uncles.' It was a miracle that the children did not innocently give the game away to their friends at school, but by 1941 even quite young children were taught to be very careful about what they said to anyone outside the family.

One day a serious problem arose for the Koumans. A bomb fell just across the road without exploding and everyone in the street had to be evacuated until it could be made safe. This was impossible for the Jews because they could not go out of the house in daylight. Neighbours would see them and a Nazi might hear about it. Before the Koumans family left their house the burgemeester, J. H. E. baron van Nagell, who was privy to their secret, arrived and advised them to hide the Jews in the cellar, where the heating for the nursery was housed. This they did. As soon as the bomb was made safe and the all-clear was given, everyone returned home and the Jews came up from the cellar.

The Koumans' luck held for over a year. Then they must have been betrayed because, without warning, the house was surrounded and all the Jews there were arrested. The Koumans' six-year-old son was thrown down the stairs because the Germans thought he was a Jewish child. All the Jews were sent to Auschwitz and only one of them survived. Wim Koumans was sent to Sachsenhausen concentration camp, and Anna was left to look after her children and to run the nursery business single-handed.

My grandfather sheltered a Jewish lady in the house in which he lived with my aunt. She came in November 1942 and stayed until the war was over. The next-door neighbour was a Nazi, one of the few in my country to be executed after the war, so he was just about the worst neighbour one could have. Nevertheless, if my grandfather was gardening the Nazi would talk to him over the fence, all nice and neighbourly. My grandfather often told him: 'You will regret this one day. Hitler will never win.'

Before the war neighbours had walked freely into one another's houses – nothing was ever locked. The practice could not be changed when the Jewish diver came, so my grandfather and aunt had to be on the alert all the time. Dutch houses have very large windows, with net curtains and heavier curtains that are normally never drawn – in the blackout at night, of course, they had to be – and if the Jewish lady went into the front room during the day she could be seen from the street. My aunt solved this problem by keeping the net curtains closed, but this was, of course, remarked upon by all the neighbours. My aunt explained: 'Drawing curtains is a sign of mourning. I am mourning because my country is occupied, and I have made a vow that they will stay closed until the war is over.' Everyone in the street thought it was a marvellous gesture. Even so, my grandfather and aunt had constantly to be careful. For example, one day they had to go to a funeral in another town and were going to be away all day. My father had to go to their house to 'diver-sit', otherwise any callers who came to the door might have heard the lavatory being flushed, or some other noise, and then have wondered why nobody answered the bell. Had the old man been taken ill, perhaps? They might have raised the alarm and found the diver.

Sometimes people had to rely on their wits to get through a difficult situation. One day there was a house-to-house search for Jews in Doorn and a lady whom everyone called Aunt Eef had ten Jews in her house. Somebody some streets away managed to warn her. As her house was on the edge of a wood, she quickly told her guests to go and hide there. Unfortunately one of the women was blind and she would have hampered the others if she had gone with them. The blind woman came from the Province of Limburg, in the south of the country, where people among themselves speak a local dialect that is difficult for others to understand. Aunt Eef put the woman in bed and told her to act as if she was ill. When Aunt Eef opened the door to the Nazi who was going to search her house, she heard that he had Limburg intonation in his speech. Immediately she said, 'How very nice to see you. I have a guest who is ill in bed and I am sure she would love to speak to someone in her own language.' She took him to the woman's bedroom after he had searched the rest of the house and the two people from Limburg had a pleasant chat in their own dialect. The Nazi never noticed that she was Jewish and forgot to ask for her identity card.

There was always the danger that a house would be searched all of a sudden. At night it was difficult to get away, because of the curfew, and people who were in the street without a permit would be arrested. Most people took precautions and built a hiding-place in their house – for example, by making space under the floorboards or by fitting a false wall in a cupboard.

Mr and Mrs Hirsch, who lived in Driebergen, received the official letter telling them that they had to go to Amsterdam in August 1941. They left by train, in a carriage labelled 'Reserved for 50 Jews'. On arrival in Amsterdam they had to live in one of the Jewish quarters. In February 1942 friends offered to take them back to Driebergen to go into hiding. They decided to wait another two days before going. On the second day a policeman came with an SS man to round them up. They were told to get ready and while Mr Hirsch came down the stairs with a suitcase the police constable heard Mrs Hirsch crying.

'How old is your wife?' he asked.

'Sixty-six,' Mr Hirsch replied.

'Is she ill?'

'Yes.'

The policeman waited until the SS man had disappeared into another house and then said to Mr Hirsch, 'Go back inside quickly to your wife. There won't be another round-up in this street for the next couple of days.'

Mr Hirsch thanked him and went back to his wife.

Naturally the Hirsches asked their friends to come and fetch them without delay. This, however, was easier said than done. Jews were not allowed to travel. At any time people could be stopped in the street or while travelling on a train. Non-Jews could then produce their identity card and, provided they were not people the Germans were looking for, all was well. But Jewish people had that letter 'J' on their cards so immediately they would be arrested unless they had a special permit for their journey.

Those who were helping the Jews evolved a system for moving them. In the street a guide would walk ahead of his or her charges. If the guide was stopped because of a road-block, the others would try to go back and hope that the guide would find them again later. If they reached the station safely, the guide would buy the tickets and look to see if there were any checks being made before passengers could go on to the platform. If that looked safe enough they could all get on the train. That was when the real danger started, as you never knew if papers would be checked while travelling. Obviously you could not get off between stations.

The Hirsches were lucky; they arrived safely in Driebergen and all through the war they stayed with the two seamstresses who had worked for them before they went to Amsterdam. The house was very small, but that did not matter as they were as safe as they could be in such circumstances and were thankful. Friends moved the floorboards beneath the carpet under a couch. A hole was made just big enough for two people to hide in. Whenever there was danger they got into their hole. Mr Hirsch kept a diary. One of his friends collected the pages regularly and hid them. A copy of this diary is now in the Imperial War Museum in London. It does not bear thinking about what would have happened if the Germans had ever found the diary.

Divers

So many groups of people were now helping others to go into hiding that a few of them decided to organise this nationally. Not unnaturally in a country criss-crossed by dykes and waterways, people who had to go into hiding were called 'divers', and on 25 November 1942 the 'National Organisation for Assistance to Divers', abbreviated to LO, the initial letters of the first two Dutch words, was founded at a meeting at the house of a furniture-shop owner in Driebergen. This was attended by twenty-one people, who included the Revd Slomp from Heemse, near the German border. This meeting took place in great secrecy and of course nothing could be put in writing. It was arranged that every Province would have a leader. The Provinces were divided into districts, which would each have a leader, and within each district the towns and villages would have a local leader, who would see to it that addresses for people in hiding were found in his or her area. The leader had to provide the divers with ration cards, identity cards and, if necessary, money for the host family. People who were not well off could not otherwise afford to have another two or three people staying with them, often for months or years.

It took several months for the LO to be fully operational throughout the country, but it eventually became the largest of all the Resistance organisations. The Driebergen LO was built up through the trade association contacts of the furniture-shop owner, so in many other towns the local section also met at the homes of furnishers. In the Province of Utrecht some members belonged to a basketball team – as I did, playing as a junior. Before the war we got to know players from teams we played against in other towns. Now these players were contacted to recruit them for the Resistance. Most

Resistance members were 'friends of friends' – a convenient and relatively safe way to recruit because we could trust one another, but, of course, such links could also prove to be dangerous if the Nazis ever made the connection between people. Most of the Resistance cells consisted of not much more than half a dozen people, because the fewer you knew the safer it was. What you didn't know you couldn't tell. I often felt that I knew far too much, because I worked with several different groups and part of my work was liaison. Consequently I knew far too many contact addresses. This added to my normal anxieties.

The Revd Slomp, one of the founders of the LO, had preached against the Nazi ideology before the war, telling people what was happening in Germany. The Germans knew this through their spies and tried to arrest him, but he went into hiding. He then travelled all over the country, preaching wherever he happened to be, using a different name. One of his favourite sermons was on Exodus 1: 15–20, which tells the story of two midwives who were ordered by the Pharaoh of Egypt to kill all male children born to Hebrew women. The midwives refused to do so. By this means the Revd Slomp conveyed the message to the congregation that they too should disobey the enemy.

It was not long before many non-Jews also had to go into hiding. Many men were ordered to go and work in Germany but they refused to do so. To sort out who was to go where, the provincial leaders of the LO held regular meetings, usually in the vestry of a church. These meetings were called 'the stock-exchange'. Someone would say, 'Who can take a baker?' (or whatever the trade or profession might be). Someone else would then offer to help, and the person to be hidden would hear where he had to go and a meeting-place with a local guide was fixed. Later on it became too dangerous to hold such meetings and the provincial leaders then went to their districts to sort it all out. Local leaders took care of the people who were accepted by the district leader.

More persecution of the Jews
In January 1943 the Germans rounded up all 1,200 patients of a Jewish mental hospital, together with 52 nurses. They were deported to Germany and nobody survived. Quite a number of Jews were hidden in mental hospitals and immediately after this raid it was feared that the Germans would look for Jews in other such places too. In Doorn, Aunt Eef had two Jews staying with her, and their mother

was hidden in a hospital under the guise of being a patient there. Aunt Eef asked her neighbour Jeanne Beekman to go and fetch Granny. While they were travelling back, all passengers on the train had their papers thoroughly checked. The reason for this turned out to be that a German general had been shot the previous day. Jeanne had not known about this but she was a very quick-thinking person. She put Granny in a corner seat, sat forward, half in front of her, and when the German came along she gave both their identity cards to be checked. Meanwhile she told everyone that the poor woman was a patient at the local mental hospital and that she was taking her on an outing. As it was a large hospital and well known in the area, no one took any notice of the 'patient'. Fortunately Granny had a forged identity card without the letter 'J' on it, otherwise things would have turned out differently.

At the station exit a Stormtrooper was standing next to the ticket collector. He was scrutinising all the passengers. Jeanne dropped both tickets and the Stormtrooper instinctively stooped to help her pick them up. While this was happening, Jeanne gave her charge a big push to get her through this checkpoint, thanked the soldier profusely for his help and then handed the tickets to the collector. No notice was taken of the old woman. At Aunt Eef's she was happily reunited with her family.

A year later, however, Granny died of natural causes. This created a big problem, as people in hiding do not officially exist, and people who do not exist cannot be buried. In such circumstances no doctor could issue a death certificate. If he were to put the real name on a certificate, everyone else in the house would be endangered because the registrar would see the name of someone who was not registered at that address and would realise that it was someone who had been hidden. Even if the registrar could be trusted, someone else might find out – when local people see a funeral they wonder who has died. Aunt Eef had a Nazi living near by, and he might have put two and two together. It was strictly forbidden to help Jews and people who were found out were generally sent to a concentration camp.

In the end the local Resistance decided to bury Granny in the garden. They waited until dark, some of the men dug a grave, and Granny was buried with as much ceremonial as possible. One of the Jews remembered some of the prayers from Kaddish and said them, It was sad that Granny did not live to see the liberation, but the family was grateful that at the end she had been cared for by her children.

Identity cards

There were several ways of obtaining a new identity card. Volunteers of the same sex and roughly the same age could be asked to 'lose' their card. They could then go to the police, have the loss registered and obtain a replacement. In the 'lost' card the photograph would be replaced and the new owner would have to learn to write the signature that was already on the card. Replacing the photograph was not easy as the stamp of the municipality was partly over it, so this had to be carefully drawn again. There was nothing you could do about the fingerprint, but during checks in streets and trains no finger-prints were taken. If you were carrying the card and were arrested and the fingerprint was checked at the police station, there was no way you could talk your way out of it. Then, of course, the person who had supplied the card and whose name and address were on it would be in mortal danger.

Sometimes someone who worked in the council offices would give the Resistance a new card issued in the name of someone who had died in childhood. This was safe, as the new owner's own photo-graph, fingerprint and signature could be put on the card. Sometimes the Resistance broke into the council offices and took blank cards.

Some problems we had with identity cards would be laughed at today, but they were real enough at the time. For example, once I had to go a long way by bus and train to take new cards to a Jewish couple.

'Of course it is marvellous that they now have cards without the letter "J" on them,' said their hostess, 'but why couldn't they have had the same surname?'

'Well,' I replied. 'we just didn't have two blank cards, so we had to forge the cards we had, putting the divers' photos on them.'

'If the surnames aren't the same, they can't sleep in the same room, let alone in the same bed. If the Germans come in the middle of the night it will look highly suspicious if, according to their docu-ments, these two sleeping together are not married! There's nothing for it,' the hostess said: 'one of them will have to move into one of the children's rooms and my three children will have to share.'

In the summer of 1943 Jeanne Beekman herself came under sus-picion. Luckily a neighbour warned her that Germans were search-ing houses in the next street. Jeanne put both her Jewish divers into her emergency hiding-place, a space behind a concealed door behind a cupboard. That night her husband was on duty as an air-raid war-den. She had two sons, aged ten and five. As she was afraid her chil-dren would be threatened and might be persuaded to say there were other people in the house, she sent them out. She told them to go and wait in the nearby wood until she fetched them. The Germans searched from 7.30 p.m. until 11.30 p.m.

'We have been told that you have Jews staying here,' they said.

'I did have some paying guests to make some extra money,' she replied. 'But I didn't ask to see their papers. Anyway, they left some time ago. Look,' she said, 'you've probably been listening to gossip. Somebody says, "They look like Jews", and the next person says, "Perhaps they are Jews", and the next one says, "They are Jews", and that is how a story gets around. They weren't, as far as I know.'

Those were the longest four hours the family ever went through. When the Nazis were leaving they said they would return the next morning. As soon as the enemy had gone, Jeanne called the divers out of their hiding place and took them to a neighbour. There was no time to lose. Only then could she go and look for her boys. They were lying on their tummies in the dark, at the edge of the wood. They must have been very frightened, as not only did they know very well that they were out during curfew hours but they also did not know what was happening at home and if they would see their mother again. Several people in their neighbourhood had already been arrested for harbouring Jews. The ten-year-old did very well to keep his younger brother quiet and still for so long.

I join the Resistance

It was often difficult to hide small Jewish children, because they were too young to understand that they absolutely must not cry or make any noise or go outside and play. One solution was to take these children to a children's home. I was asked by a friend of our family, who worked with the local police and therefore knew when a Jewish family was in danger, to travel with these children. Many of them had dark hair and brown eyes, as I did, so at eighteen I could pretend to be their older sister. Families were much larger in those days and there was often quite an age gap between the eldest and the youngest.

The first time, I had to collect a three-year-old-boy. It was heart-breaking, and I still look on this as one of the worst jobs I ever had to do. He did not want to leave his mother, and the mother did not know the stranger who was taking her child away. We got on the train without mishap but half-way through the journey the boy started to cry. 'I don't want to come with you,' he kept saying loudly, 'I want my Mummy.' It was a non-corridor train and at one of the stations where the train had stopped somebody wearing a Nazi badge had got on.

My heart was in my mouth. I was very frightened. I tried telling the little boy a story, but that did not work. In desperation I started chatting up a woman sitting opposite me. I told her that the boy was crying because his mother was ill and had to go into hospital. I was taking him for the time being to an auntie, but he didn't understand and didn't want to go. This explained his unhappiness satisfactorily enough, and as luck would have it the woman had recently been in hospital herself, and started talking about all her adventures there. Soon everyone was interested in her tales and attention was drawn away from the little boy and me. We completed our journey safely but I am sure the child went on missing his mother. I never knew who he was, or if he and his parents survived the war.

Taking a child away from his mother was the most traumatic experience, and the awfulness of what was going on was brought home to me dramatically. I knew then that I had to commit myself and do something positive. Becoming part of the Resistance seemed the logical and natural step to take. I made contact through the friend who had asked me to take the little boy to the home. From then on I took children to safe addresses if the occasion arose.

A few months later something must have gone wrong and my name was mentioned, I do not know by whom. My friend warned me that I had better disappear, so I said goodbye to my family – my parents, of course, knew what I was doing, though not the details – and I left home for a few weeks. As no one came to arrest me during that time it seemed safe to return home, which I did.

Once I became involved I just went on doing things, often simply by meeting friends and being asked to help. Some of us, such as Ans and Oets (Klaas van Middelkoop) and Paul Bos, belonged to the same basketball team. Jaap Jongejan (whom you will hear about in chapter 2) knew my family because he had been at boarding school with my cousin. My parents had put him up for a while when he had to become a diver. One way and another there is a connection somewhere with all the people whose stories I tell.

In 1943, looking after divers and taking ration cards and identity papers and other items to people for the Resistance was not a full-time job. By 1944, however, when the fighting was coming nearer, we had to provide daily intelligence and distribute weapons and explosives. This was a full-time job, seven days a week, and there was no question of leading a normal, everyday life. My father supported me financially, but I expect the Resistance would have found money for me if it had been necessary. Many people gave money to the

Resistance but we were not paid for what we did, as the foreign agents were. I did not have to buy food. People would give me a meal whenever I arrived at a safe house, although eventually, towards the end, they sometimes had to say, 'Sorry, we have no food to offer you today.' I remember being very hungry during the last two or three months of the occupation, along with everyone else.

In March 1943 the Germans decreed that all students had to sign a declaration that they would be loyal to the Germans. Most of them refused. Unfortunately this was not the end of it. In May they were told to report to a labour camp. Nobody knew what to expect, so most of them did not go. Three thousand students did report and these were promptly sent to Germany to work. All the others immediately wanted to go into hiding. The next day all men between the ages of eighteen and thirty-five were ordered to go to the labour exchange, where they were given a job in Germany. Those who did not want to go also had to be hidden. A month earlier all former military personnel had had to report to the Germans so that they could become POWs. Most of these did not go either and they also had to be hidden. This all meant there was a lot of work for the Resistance to do.

2

Summer 1943 to 'Mad Tuesday' 1944

Hiding Jewish children

In August 1943 a ten-year-old Jewish boy who was hidden in Driebergen was betrayed. When one person, or a few people, were to be arrested, the Germans would order the Dutch police to do it. The Germans carried out the mass arrests and sudden raids. So in this instance the people who were hiding the boy were told in advance that a policeman would collect him the next morning and take him to Amsterdam. They were ordered not to tell anyone, and because the police were involved and not the Germans the family were lucky enough not to be arrested themselves. Fortunately they took no notice of the injunction to say nothing and they told Jaap Jongejan, a member of the Resistance. Jaap was a school teacher who had been a corporal in the Dutch army in May 1940. He was now in hiding because he had not followed the German order that all soldiers had to report to be taken to a POW camp.

Jaap decided to kidnap the Jewish boy. In those days the trains from Driebergen went alternately to Amsterdam and Rotterdam. Passengers for Amsterdam who travelled on the Rotterdam train had to change trains in Utrecht. The policeman who had to collect the boy agreed to take him on a Rotterdam train. Jaap bought two tickets and went ahead on an earlier train, so that he would be waiting on the platform when the train with the boy and policeman arrived. He took the child and left the station with him. The policeman was a marvellous actor. To give them as much of a start as possible he walked up and down the platform asking passengers, 'Have you seen a ten-year-old boy dressed in grey shorts and a blue pullover?' Nobody had, of course. He then went to the station-master and asked for an announcement to be made over the loud-speakers, saying that a child had got lost. When that did not work, the message was broadcast again. Only after that did he ring his chief to tell him that because of the crowds he had become separated from the boy. When he got back he managed to tell his story so convincingly that no disciplinary action was taken. The boy was taken to another town far away from Driebergen.

A few weeks later Jaap was arrested – no one ever found out why – and he was sent to a German concentration camp. Months after the war was over, the Red Cross wrote to his parents that he had died there at the age of twenty-five.

Also in Driebergen there were two middle-aged sisters, Bep and Joe Holst, who were running a children's home. They were known to the children as Aunt Bep and Aunt To. Their house was opposite my family's home, on the outskirts of the town, almost on the edge of a large wood. A stream ran down the middle of the road, with small pedestrian bridges every 200 metres (219 yards). Because of this stream, people living in the road never had Germans billeted on them. The Germans did not like a road where they could not cross quickly from one side to the other. All these factors made the sisters feel fairly safe in taking in Jewish children, who were all given new names. They had it dinned into them never to mention their own name again. They were also told not to talk about their parents while they were playing in the garden.

Aunt Bep had long hair which she wore in a bun. She was the stronger of the two. She made the decisions, did the cooking and organised everything. Aunt To suffered from headaches and had to have a lot of rest. Both of them were marvellous with the children.

Every afternoon – weather permitting – they went to the woods where the children could play. There was small lake in one of the woods and this was a favourite spot. They played there for hours. The small children went in push-chairs as they could not manage the long walks.

The aunts checked that the children brushed their teeth morning and evening and they had to show their nails in the evening to check that they were clean after playing in the woods.

All the children had a small task to do in the house: helping with the dusting, washing up, clearing the table after a meal. They said grace before and after meals. On Sundays they had a specially good tablecloth and used the Sunday dinner service. This made it a special day, like having a party. The children had to be extra careful when they carried the dirty plates of the Sunday service to the kitchen at the end of each course. It made it all so cheerful.

At night, the aunts tucked the children in and read stories. They also had a children's Bible and read simple stories from it. They played a lot of board games, like ludo, and older children had to practise their writing. The children received much love and care while they were with their 'aunts'.

There were between eight and twelve children in the house. A teacher from a local school went there from time to time to give the older ones lessons and set them some homework, so that when the war was over they would be able to go back to school without having lost too much time. One of the boys was working for the Dutch equivalent of the eleven-plus grammar school entrance examination. He came to our house three times a week so that I could give him extra lessons, until his parents took him away from the home to be with them again.

On 15 November 1943 the Germans raided the sisters' house. Perhaps they were betrayed. Perhaps there had been some careless talk. Nobody will ever know. The sisters were put in the kitchen and the children were forbidden to go to them. The house was searched and the children were asked their names. The eldest, Nelleke, was ten years old; the youngest was a baby. Nelleke refused to admit that her new name was not her own name, but she was not believed. In the end they were all bundled into a Black Maria to be taken to Amsterdam, with Nelleke holding the baby on her lap. When they got into the van Aunt Bep said, 'Let's sing.' They sang 'Praise, my soul, the King of Heaven' and other hymns. On arrival in Amsterdam the children were separated from their 'aunts'. Aunt Bep said to Nelleke that she was the eldest and now had to look after the other children. All the children were taken to Camp Westerbork, which was a transit camp in the east of the country where the Jews waited for their deportation. Every week a packed train left there for Germany. Those who were not on the list waited another week, hoping they would again not be on the list. Most Jews from Westerbork were sent to Auschwitz. Jews who had become Christians were generally sent to a concentration camp in Theresienstadt, which was not an extermination camp as Auschwitz was.

When Nelleke's parents, who were hiding in another town, heard that their daughter had been arrested they tried to get her declared a Christian. A friend of theirs went to a minister and asked if he would issue a baptismal certificate in Nelleke's name. The minister showed his visitor the blank certificates and said that his conscience forbade him to issue such a certificate to someone who had not been baptised. He then made an excuse and left the room. His visitor took the certificates and quickly left the minister's house. He put Nelleke's name on one of the certificates and took it to the Germans in Westerbork. Because of this certificate Nelleke was sent to Theresienstadt and survived the war. Seven of the other children died in Auschwitz, including Jacky, the boy to whom I had been giving extra lessons, for he and his parents were also arrested soon afterwards. Even now he still haunts my thoughts. I see him cheerfully coming to me with his books, happy when I gave him good marks, and waving goodbye to me. All this to end up in a gas chamber in Auschwitz.

Aunt Bep and Aunt To were sent to the concentration camp at Vught. This camp was in the south of the Netherlands. On 15 January 1944 the Germans pushed seventy-four women into a room measuring 4 metres by 2.24 metres (about 13 feet by 7 feet) in a concrete bunker there – a modern equivalent of the Black Hole of Calcutta. When they opened the door after fourteen hours, Aunt Bep and nine other women had died. Aunt To survived but never recovered from this terrible experience. She spent the next six months in the camp hospital and was then released.

Sometimes help arrived unexpectedly when you were in a difficult situation. A family in Maarsbergen had two Jewish boys, aged eight and ten, hidden in their house. One day they noticed a Nazi walking past their house several times. Neighbours had also commented on this. The family was worried that he might have caught a glimpse of the boys and they decided to move them. Chris Blom, a member of the local Resistance, arranged for a family in Eindhoven to take the boys. He put them on his bicycle and rode to a nearby station to take the train to Utrecht. He did not dare to use the local station. Chris had arranged with a member of the Resistance in Eindhoven that a guide would pick them up and take the small fugitives from Utrecht to Eindhoven. In Utrecht the guide did not arrive. This was not unusual as trains often did not run on time. A train could be bombed and would cause so much delay that connections were missed. Chris felt rather conspicuous standing on the platform with the two boys without boarding any of the trains that stopped there. After some time a railwayman came up to him and said casually, 'I have a feeling that you are in trouble. Why don't you put those boys in the mail cart?' A large cart was standing on the platform waiting for the mailbags which were coming on a much later train. Chris gratefully jumped at the chance and helped the boys into the cart, which was so high that they were completely hidden from anyone on the platform. Fortunately the guide turned up in the end. The boys survived the war but their father was killed in Auschwitz.

Raiding food offices

Before the war started, the Dutch Government had made all the preparations in case food rationing should become necessary. Each citizen had received a card divided up into little squares. On presentation of this card a ration card would be issued and one of the squares would be marked. The Dutch Government had provided large stores of food so that rationing seemed a long way off. However, the Germans stole the stores and sent them to Germany, necessitating food rationing for us. This created a problem for people who were in hiding. They did not only need a safe address but also food. The Resistance now had to work out how to provide ration cards for all these people on a regular basis, as each month a new one was issued.

The only way to do this was to raid food offices and take the cards. Small action groups of six to eight men were formed. They made contact with someone who worked in the food office to find out when the new cards would arrive, usually shortly before they were to be issued. The group then went to the office at a quiet time of day and told everyone present – staff and any visitors who happened to be there – to put up their hands. They had to lock everyone up so that the staff could truthfully say that they had been unable to prevent the raid as the men were armed and had taken them prisoner. The cards were taken out of the safe and put in a waiting car. Everything had to be done very quickly. Driving a car was dangerous, as only Germans and people with a special permit were allowed to use one. The cards were given to members of the LO, who knew how many were needed in every town. Local representatives took them to the people who were sheltering divers. Later on, these groups were organised nationally into the Landelijke Knokploegen (LKP); in that way no two groups would raid the same office at the same time.

Although raids were carried out by men on bicycles, the best way was to use a car. When the Germans confiscated Dutch cars early in the occupation some people managed to hide theirs. A number of cars were secreted in large holes in a wood. This way the Germans could not use them, but neither, unfortunately, could the Resistance. The solution was to conceal the car in a hiding place that was both large enough and sufficiently accessible to enable a driver to take the car in and out quickly. In the town of Doorn an enterprising coach-

W.L.A. du Celliée Muller, 1887–1942

Sergeant De Beus, 1893–1961

Left: Aunt To
J.M. Holst, 1894–1980

Right: Aunt Bep
L.E. Holst, 1887–1944

Concealing a car

builder made a vertical lift-bridge inside a coal shed. A car driven on to the bridge could be lowered, using a hydraulic system, until it disappeared under the floor. Bags of coal were stacked together on the floor so that the place looked like an ordinary coal shed. The car could be taken out and driven away in a very short time. There were also bunks under the floor so that three people could sleep there in times of danger. The car was never discovered and was used by the Resistance.

In August 1944 the Resistance planned to raid the Doorn food office. As there had been several raids in neighbouring towns already, an armed policeman was now placed on duty to guard each office. In Doorn, Sergeant De Beus worked with the Resistance, so the raid had to be done on a day when he was on duty. The sergeant always tried to warn people who were sheltering Jews when their house was going to be searched if he happened to hear about it beforehand. He used to send his small daughter to those families with the message: 'Daddy says you should go and walk your dog.'

The best day for the raid did not coincide with Sergeant De Beus's guard duty, so he had to make a pretext to change his rota with a colleague. In the end it took the raiders longer than anticipated to reach the office. One of the employees said to the secretary, 'I can't understand what is happening. They should have been here by now.' At last the raiders arrived. De Beus did not use his gun, so they entered without any trouble. Everyone present dutifully put their hands up and they were all locked in the cellar. The loot was 11,646 ration cards and 15,668 other coupons.

Sergeant De Beus was now in a difficult position. As he would never have been able to explain why he had not acted to prevent the raid, he would most certainly have been held responsible. The only option open to him was to disappear with the raiders and remain in hiding until the war was over. His salary was still paid, as no one reported that he was not at work. Had this not been the case, there was an organisation that provided regular pay to families where the father was in hiding. This came to millions of guilders, which the Dutch Government repaid after the war.

The staff in the food office waited until the raiders had had ample time to make their get-away. Then they kicked a panel out of the cellar door and reported the loss of the cards. As soon as the burgemeester was notified and had given the police the order to investigate, he got on his bicycle and rode to the De Beus family to warn them to clear the house of anything that could link them to the Resistance.

Forced labour

To prevent the Allies from invading the Continent the Germans built the Atlantic wall, which ran from Norway to Spain. It was a huge defence line and, to their annoyance, building it took much longer than they had anticipated. They decided that the unskilled work could be done by Dutchmen. In addition to that they wanted manholes dug along all major roads away from the coast. If the road was bombed or shelled, a soldier could jump into one of these holes and be safe. The Germans decided that Dutchmen up to the age of forty-five should dig them.

Some men were able to go into hiding or otherwise avoid working for the Germans. This was much easier for non-Jews than it had been for the Jews. There was nothing on their identity card to indicate that they should be in Germany because they were either a student or a soldier. Men between the ages of eighteen and thirty-five were supposed to have reported to the labour exchange for work in Germany. However, there were exemptions – for example, if you were a fireman, a priest, a farmer or a doctor. Also some men were declared unfit for work in Germany. Those people were given an *Ausweis*, a German permit. This document stated that they had failed their medical examination or that they were necessary for work in their own country. Needless to say, the Resistance managed to get hold of blank permits, fill them in with the required details and forge the German signatures. With such a permit a man could travel reasonably safely. He could not, of course, stay in his home town, because friends and neighbours would realise that he should not be there but in Germany.

The men who were sent to Germany had to work in factories or on farms, so that the Germans they replaced could go and join the army. No occupying power is supposed to use people in an occupied country in such a way that they end up working for the enemy. So all these measures were against international law, but the Germans did not worry about that. The war was not going very well for them and they needed every able-bodied man.

At first burgemeesters were asked to direct men to go and dig the manholes in the roads. In the Province of Brabant eight burgemeesters refused to do so. They were sent to a concentration camp and only one of them survived. The Germans decided to go to the council offices and scrutinise the registers, which were kept there. The burgemeester of Leersum (population 2,700) refused to let them do so and he was jailed, as was the town clerk. A quisling was appointed burgemeester. The burgemeester in Doorn was 'lucky'. The military Ortskommandant liked and respected him. The burgemeester spoke faultless German and when the Germans got nasty he was able to reply in the same vein. The Ortskommandant summoned the burgemeester to his office and kept him there for most of the day. In the meantime his henchmen looked through the registers to find men of the required age group. When they had finished, the Ortskommandant told the burgemeester what had happened. He said: 'I knew you would refuse and I did not want to have to arrest you.'

In towns and villages where no searches of the registers had yet been made, it became necessary for the records of men up to forty-five years old to 'disappear'. In Langbroek, a small, scattered farming community of only 1,500 inhabitants, Harry Hello, a member of the Resistance, worked in the council office. As the town clerk had a German wife, it seemed too risky to ask for his co-operation. Harry knew that the town clerk always took the keys to the office home with him. Curfew started at 8 p.m., so early one evening five mem-'ers of an action group from outside Langbroek, led by Jan de Groot (whose real name was Freerk Postmus), rang the doorbell at the town clerk's house. As soon as he opened the door, the men entered and locked him and his wife in a bedroom. Two of them stayed in the house while the others went to the council office with the keys.

The two in the house had not been there long when the doorbell rang. They looked at each other anxiously. Was the visitor friend or foe? They opened the door cautiously, to find one of the local farmers standing there. Because there was no bank in Langbroek the town clerk acted as agent for one in the nearest town. This helped farmers, who were too busy during the day to go to the bank but who could call on the town clerk at his home in the evening, before the curfew started.

'Oh,' said the farmer. 'I wanted to see the town clerk. Is he in? What's going on? Who are you?'

The men did not answer that question. 'Come in – bring your bike inside,' one of them said. 'The town clerk is upstairs. I'll take you to him. You'll have to stay with him, as we can't let you go home until we go ourselves. And please don't ask questions.'

They went upstairs, where the farmer greeted the town clerk and his wife and said, 'I've come to do my banking. What's going on?'

'Good evening,' the town clerk answered calmly. 'Well, you see, there is obviously a raid on at the council office. They have taken my keys. These men are keeping us here until it is over. They won't hurt us if we don't do anything stupid. Look,' he said, turning to the two men, 'if you will allow my wife to go to my study, she can fetch the books and cash from the safe – the key to that is downstairs. Then we can conduct our business and our friend here will be able to go home before the curfew starts, won't he? You will be gone before then too?'

The men agreed, and one of them went with the woman to make sure she did not try to run away or give a signal to anyone. When they returned, the farmer conducted his business and they all waited.

Meanwhile the other Resistance men had gone to the council office and entered the building. Within half an hour they had carried away the relevant registers and a number of blank identity cards. They buried the registers in a tin box in a garden in Doorn, took the car back to its hiding-place – a large haystack – and returned the keys to the town clerk. The farmer left on his bicycle, assuring the men that, if anyone asked, he had never seen them, and the action group members slipped quickly away.

Langbroek had a policeman, Sergeant Bouw, who helped the Resistance whenever he could. If they had planned something, he was told to take the evening off. So he had done just that during the raid on the council office. The day following the raid Bouw had to make a report. He interviewed Harry, who had to check which registers had been taken. He did this very conscientiously. It was a good piece of acting, both men knowing exactly what had happened and who had done it. The town clerk must have decided that discretion was the better part of valour and did not press for further investigation.

Sergeant Bouw was involved again at the end of August 1944, when two men were arrested by the Germans in Doorn. They were put in the lock-up at the police station for the night, awaiting transport to Utrecht the next morning. That night, purely by chance, Sergeant Bouw had changed duties with his Doorn colleague. An action group arrived to liberate the two men. Since Bouw was supposed to be guarding the prisoners, he suggested the action group should knock him out so that he could not be held responsible. As the first blow with the butt of a revolver did not have the desired effect, Bouw told them to hit him harder. This they did, and with the keys which Bouw had given the group beforehand they opened the door of the cell and released the men, who were taken to a safe address. Bouw stayed unconscious for longer than had been planned. He suffered from concussion and was off duty for a month. His superiors were totally convinced.

It was always an advantage to have somebody in the council offices who worked with the Resistance and could change data in a register or insert the assumed names of people who were in hiding. After the war the Resistance leader in Doorn even received two summonses for the first general election: one in his own name and one in the name that had been on his forged identity card.

Girl couriers

A major problem for the Resistance was to find a fair way of distributing ration cards. Sometimes members had not had a raid in their locality, while others had had several raids in their region. Cards could not be sent through the post as that would have been too dangerous. The men could not travel without running great risks. Although they had very good permits and identity cards, these were, after all, forgeries, and young men in particular were likely to be stopped and checked. It was much safer for girls to travel with ration cards, identity cards, permits, and so on. Soon we were travelling long distances, taking cards from places where they had too many to others where they did not have enough. One of the dangers was that sometimes luggage was searched. Another was the journey itself. From 1943 onwards the British attacked locomotives from the air to destroy as many of them as possible. At first the planes flew over the train a few times as a warning. Passengers had time to get off the train and run as far away as they could. By 1944 there were no such niceties: casualties occurred among both passengers and railway personnel as the trains were shot at without warning. Eventually the railway company put an extra man on the locomotive. He had to stick his head out and watch for planes throughout the journey. When he spotted one, the driver stopped the train and everyone ran for their lives. There was a rumour that a pilot could not see which end of the train was the front and which was the rear. Consequently, everybody tried to get into the middle of the train, which made those coaches overcrowded.

Sometimes tense situations arose that – in retrospect at least – turned out to be quite amusing, in so far as the Germans unwittingly helped us, or we hoodwinked them. We were all living on our wits. I once had to fetch 600 ration cards from Boxmeer, south of Nijmegen in Limburg, which in those days involved making a very long journey. Unfortunately the man who asked me to go did not know either the name of the people concerned or their precise address, though he knew where the house was. He drew me a map showing the way from the station to their home, which I followed exactly. I rang the doorbell and, to my horror, a German opened the door. I went hot and cold all over. I really thought that the address had been blown and I had had it. The German, however, was very kind. Before I could say anything (we always took the precaution of noting the name of a neighbour a few doors away whom we could pretend to be looking for – it was customary for householders to put their names on the outside of their houses) he immediately said, 'I expect you are looking for Mr So-and-So. We requisitioned his house this morning, but I can tell you where he has gone.' Thanks to the German I now knew my contact's name and was able to find the house without difficulty. I left with the cards, which the householder had luckily been able to hide in his own belongings when he was moved out. He too had had to be quick-witted.

My troubles were not over yet, however. On the way back I had to take a bus, and half-way through the journey the bus was stopped, everyone was told to show their identity card and the Germans started to search all the luggage. There was no way I was going to be able to explain what I was doing travelling with 600 ration cards! But my luck held. A few weeks earlier my best friend, Ank Prevo, who was also a courier, had advised me to keep a photograph of an SS man in uniform in my handbag. Ank knew someone who had a cousin who had joined the SS and she gave me a copy of his photograph. This seemed the right moment to try it out and see if it helped. When the German unfolded my identity card, the photograph fell out. I smiled as sweetly as I could. 'That's my boyfriend,' I said. 'He's fighting on the Russian front.' When I started to open my bag, he told me not to bother. It was heart-warming that I got quite a few dirty looks from my fellow travellers when the bus was allowed to continue. In any event, although my heart had been pounding and my mouth had gone dry, I was now feeling very pleased with myself. I had got away with it! I took some of the ration cards to Ank in Amerongen, where she was my local contact. She had the job of distributing the cards in the town.

In every town and village the Resistance had addresses where members could be contacted. The safest were those where many people called in the normal course of the day. In Leersum the contact was Jans Lagemaat's grocer's shop, and in Driebergen a bank. Resistance workers blended inconspicuously with customers. In Driebergen the bank had a connecting door with the manager's house, so if there were no customers you could enter his house via the bank. If there were people about, you could take a long time to fill in a form and wait until the coast was clear. In the bank was a safe, hired out to somebody who did not exist. That safe was used if ration cards, blank permits and such things had to be kept for a while. People whose house functioned as a contact point for the Resistance were always at risk, since their addresses were known to many. Single people could go somewhere else if they thought they were in danger, but a mother could not leave her children; nor could a farmer leave his livestock.

Sabotage

After the successful landings in Normandy on 6 June 1944, everyone hoped that the war would soon be over. The action groups made a plan of campaign to help the Allied armies during the liberation of the Netherlands. A National Sabotage Commander was appointed and he made an overall plan to sabotage the railway lines. Enough damage had to be done to prevent the Germans from using the railways but not so much that the Allies would be precluded from using them if they needed to. At the beginning of September our Government-in-exile ordered us to commit acts of sabotage and called for a railway strike. The Resistance now became an armed Resistance, with weapons and explosives being flown in from Britain. On the night of 3 September sabotage action started all over the country. U-shaped staves 35 cm (just over 1 foot) in length were screwed on to the tracks to derail the trains. The ever-resourceful Doorn coachbuilder made them in such a way that one stave would push the train to the left while the stave on the opposite side of the rail would push the train up. He sent them by rail in boxes labelled 'spare parts for tractors'.

In some places sections of the rails were unscrewed or explosives were used. Girl couriers carried the explosives and other things to the required places. Because it was risky for the men to go out in daylight, in September 1944 our sabotage expert taught me how to blow up a bridge, a railway line, or whatever was targeted, and I went round the different groups with the explosives, cords and detonators, showing the men in turn how to use them. Different colours were used in cords and detonators to indicate different speeds at which the bombs could be exploded.

As all the work had to be done in the dark, it was necessary to sabotage tracks that ran outside the towns and villages. In Driebergen the railway went through a wood. An action group built a shelter there where ten to fifteen men could stay. A fir-tree hid the entrance and when this tree was pushed aside you could go down a ladder into the shelter. The fir had to be replaced by another every so often as, having been uprooted, each one died. The great advantage was that the group could sabotage the railway at night and need not worry about being out during the curfew. The sabotage was so successful that the Germans decided to punish the whole town. Local men were forced to patrol the line which of course hampered our operations because we could not put these men at risk by blowing up the line anywhere near them.

One of the men who was forced to patrol the railway line was a teacher at the school my sister Ank attended. When some of the pupils heard that he had to go and do this one afternoon after school, six of them decided to go there to cheer him up. They walked through the woods but, before they reached the line, they were stopped by a stormtrooper. They were now in trouble, because a current 'gathering banning order' forbade more than five people to be outside together – and apparently it applied to children too. They were severely told off and asked what they were doing. Because they were under fifteen years old they had no identity cards, so they had their names and addresses taken. They were ordered to go home at once – and they were made to split up into two groups!

Our railway line was an important one, as trains from Utrecht went through Driebergen to go via Arnhem to Germany. There were not enough Nazis to keep an eye on everybody, so opportunities were taken for some spur-of-the-moment sabotage. One night a long train with brand-new cars came along the track. Because of the danger of obstruction the Germans ran the trains very slowly. The men along the line threw stones at the cars until all the windows were smashed. The locals must have been more than a little annoyed when that train arrived at its destination in Germany.

'Mad Tuesday'

Paris was liberated on 23 August and Brussels on Sunday, 3 September 1944. On that Sunday the BBC broadcast a message from General Dwight D. Eisenhower to the Dutch people, which began: 'The hour of your liberation is now very near.' The next day Radio Orange, which provided daily news broadcasts from the BBC studio in London, made the following announcement: 'According to official sources, British troops have reached Breda. According to unofficial sources, they have already penetrated much farther into the Netherlands.'

It was understandable that the Dutch people thought that they would be liberated in only a matter of days. Everywhere in the south of the country people left their homes, often carrying or wearing the national colours, and went to look for the liberators. People in Rotterdam, which is only about 65 km (39 miles) from Breda, went to the outskirts of the city to wait for the first Allied tanks to arrive along the Breda–Rotterdam road. In the evening everyone had to give up and go home again before the curfew started. All that day and next one, Tuesday, 5 September, the wildest rumours were going round. Nobody had seen the Allied troops but many people had spoken to someone who had done, but they never came and the disappointment was indescribable.

The members of the Dutch Nazi Party also thought that the liberation was imminent. They were afraid of being imprisoned once the Dutch Government-in-exile returned. Many of them decided to flee to Germany, leaving most of their possessions behind. On that Tuesday there was complete chaos on the roads. The Nazis travelled to the nearest railway station on carts, bicycles, carrier tricycles or any other available means of transport. Extraordinarily, given their military situation at the time, the Germans put on extra trains to take more than 60,000 Nazis to Germany. Because of all the chaos and the confusion of this day, 5 September 1944 was later called 'Mad Tuesday'.

It was also a sad day for the Dutch members of the Resistance who were being held in a concentration camp at Vught, a town near Breda. On this day and the next, 2,800 men and 650 women were transported to German concentration camps, the men to Sachsenhausen and the women to Ravensbrück. This was a terrible development, as the liberators were only a short distance away. Many of those who were transported subsequently died in Germany. Four members of the Resistance who tried to sabotage the railway line to prevent the trains containing prisoners from going to Germany were caught and executed. During the first six days of September 1944 the Germans executed 133 prisoners. They did not bother to tell the town clerk about all of these, which caused great difficulties with the issue of death certificates later on. Many families did not hear what had happened to their husbands and fathers until long after the war. Some of them are not sure of their fate even now.

Also on 5 September the Dutch Government-in-exile decided to amalgamate into one organisation three of the Resistance organisations, the Ordedienst (OD), the Raad van Verzet (RVV), and the Landelijke Knokploegen (LKP). Up to that time these had been busy independently, gathering intelligence and carrying out sabotage, raids and rescues. This new organisation, called Binnenlandse Strijdkrachten (Interior Forces of the Netherlands), shortened to BS, was regarded as an underground army. The members of the BS received military status from their own Government, and command was given to Prince Bernhard, who acted under direct orders from General Eisenhower. The 'National Organisation for Assistance to Divers' or LO to which I belonged until the summer of 1944, when I joined the LKP action groups, remained separate. Its task continued to be to care for the divers, although if necessary members would assist the BS. This certainly applied to the girl couriers. If one of us had to cycle a long way to take ration cards to another town and at the same time weapons had to go to the same place, it was very likely that we would be asked to do both jobs. I did become very involved with some of the BS groups in my area later on.

The BS divided the country into regions, each one with a regional commander. The regions were divided into districts, with a district commander. In the districts each town or village had a local commander. If there was a big job to be done, then several local groups worked together.

Before 'Mad Tuesday' all Resistance groups had been drawing up lists with names of the Nazis they intended to arrest as soon as the Germans had left. Plans had to be made about where they would be kept prisoner until better facilities became available. In Maarsbergen, which was a hamlet near Maarn, just across the forest to the east of Driebergen, there was a reform school for boys, called Valkenheide. This institution had a block with some rooms where boys could be locked up if necessary. It seemed an ideal place for a temporary jail. The school had about three hundred boys aged fourteen to twenty-one. They were taught a trade and had a choice of fourteen different ones. Alternatively they could learn to become farm labourers or gardeners, as the school also had a farm and a large garden. The governor, Mr D. Noordam, was always willing to help the Resistance. Several of his group leaders were divers who had gone into hiding to avoid having to go to work in Germany. They were provided with false papers to save them from becoming slave labour. The school had a total of eighty staff. The governor was well liked by his staff and by the boys. He was strict but fair with them. Earlier in the occupation the Germans had tried to recruit some of the older boys into the SS. Mr Noordam had stood up to the Germans and told them that they had no business with his boys, as most of them had been placed there by a Dutch law court.

Jans Lagemaat-Van den Brink, 1901–1987

D. Noordam, 1881-1944

The teacher in the shoe-repairing department, Chris Blom, was the commander of the local Resistance group. He even had a telephone link with Breda and other towns in the south. This connection had been made in broad daylight by an employee of the telephone company, who made out that he was repairing a German telephone line. Dutch telephones had long since been disconnected on German orders, but some Dutch telephone technicians had to work for the company to keep the German lines in working order.

When it was announced that the liberators were in Breda, Blom rang his contact for verification. He was told that the BBC broadcast had been a mistake and the Allies were not in fact about to arrive. Blom immediately warned all his contacts to be careful and not come out into the open as Resistance workers at this time. Unfortunately, however, some actions had already been set in train that could not now be stopped.

On 5 September some members of the Resistance, among them Mr B. C. M. van der Hoop, the leader of the OD in the area round Maarsbergen, went to the council offices in Leersum to arrest the Nazi burgemeester. They took him to Chris Blom's house. Blom rang Mr Noordam to tell him what had happened and Mr Noordam suggested that they should bring their prisoner to the lock-up at Valkenheide. Blom was not very happy about this but Mr Noordam said, 'Can't you see that they are fleeing the country everywhere? We had better lock him up.' The same day the prisoner's son called by chance on his father in the council offices. One of the officials there told him that his father had had to go out. The son then went to the pub next door, whose owner was a member of the Nazi party. The publican told him that he had seen the burgemeester with a man he did not recognise and who had later left and that his father had then gone off with Mr Van der Hoop. The son thought this was odd, so he went to ask the advice of the nearest SS commandant. The German ordered six of his men, including an officer, to go and investigate.

In the meantime the town clerk had managed to send a message to Van der Hoop to warn him that enquiries were being made. The SS arrived at Van der Hoop's house before he could warn Mr Noordam. The house was on the road from Leersum to Maarsbergen, as was Valkenheide, and luckily it was also on the edge of the forest. Van der Hoop was just able to leave via the cellar and hide under a large spruce tree before the Germans knocked on the door.

Mrs Van der Hoop was at home and she was interrogated by the SS officer-in-charge. After denying any knowledge of the whereabouts of the Nazi burgemeester she was told that if she did not inform the SS where he was all the men living on the right-hand side of the road would be shot. As that would not have been the first time the Germans had taken such terrible reprisals, she was convinced that he meant it. She was still reluctant to say what she knew, but the SS officer was persuasive and gave her his word as an officer that nobody would be harmed if she told them what they wanted to know. Eventually, unable to contemplate being responsible for the deaths of so many men if the Germans carried out their threatened executions she told them the Nazi was at Valkenheide.

Unfortunately, at about the same time something similar had happened in Wijk bij Duurstede, some distance to the south-west of Leersum. The burgemeester there was also a Nazi, and from an overheard telephone conversation the Resistance found out that he and another local Nazi were planning to flee the country. The Resistance there also thought the liberation would be only a matter of a day or two at the most, so they decided to arrest both men. They took them to farmer Van Laar, whose land bordered on the dyke of the River Rhine between Amerongen and Wijk bij Duurstede. From there they obtained the use of a car to take the two men, accompanied by their wives and a child, to Valkenheide, a distance of about 16 km (10 miles).

Jan Lagemaat was the local Resistance commander in Leersum and chief officer of the local fire brigade. He was a man with deep religious convictions and a rock-like faith in God's guiding hand. Before he went out on a mission he would always read the Bible with his group and play his favourite psalms on his harmonium. The young men would wait respectfully until he had completed this ritual.

On this occasion, he had promised to be on the road between Leersum and Valkenheide to join the others and show them the best way to the lock-up. When Jan saw the SS arrive he fled into the forest and managed to reach Valkenheide on foot. He waited there for the car from Wijk bij Duurstede. By then it was late in the evening and there was no way of warning the driver. When the car drove past Van der Hoop's house the driver saw a German car blocking the road and an SS man signalling him to stop. The driver took his foot off the accelerator so that it sounded as though he was going to stop. At the very last moment he put his foot down and drove round the roadblock. The Germans started to shoot and the Resistance men fired back. The Germans began to pursue the car. At that moment Chris Blom, who was standing 800 metres (956 yards) farther on down the road, jumped into a ditch and started shooting with his pistol in one hand and his revolver in the other. To the surprise and relief of the Resistance men, the Germans abandoned their chase. After the war, when he was questioned about it, the SS officer concerned declared that he had given up the pursuit as he had been shot at from two sides and thought the whole forest was full of partisans.

The Resistance group, when they had recovered from the shock and reached Valkenheide safely, decided there was no alternative to keeping all the prisoners at Valkenheide, as there was nowhere else they could take them. It was now 5 a.m. the next day.

Jan Lagemaat hid his gun in the forest and walked home through the trees, as that seemed safer than using the roads. Just after he had got rid of his weapon, an SS soldier stepped out from the trees and stopped him at gunpoint. He demanded to know what Jan was doing there during the curfew. Jan, reckoning that attack would be the best defence, replied as haughtily as he could: 'I am the chief officer of the local fire brigade. I am checking the forest for the Wehrmacht commander as there may be a danger of fire – it is so dry.' He added that he would appreciate it if the German would be less officious and would leave him to do his job.

'I am terribly sorry, sir,' the SS man replied politely, 'but you don't know what has been going on here all through the night.'

Luckily, neither do you, thought Jan.

SS brutality

The SS officer arrested Mrs Van der Hoop and went back to get further orders. He was sent on 7 September to free the prisoners at Valkenheide. Mr Noordam kept very cool and managed to convince the SS that he had not known anything about the people who had apparently been locked up in one of his buildings. He expressed great astonishment and concern that they were there, and the SS believed him. Everyone breathed a huge sigh of relief. Chris Blom went into hiding at a local farm. He rang Mr Noordam and advised him to do the same. Blom was afraid that the Sicherheitsdienst (SD) would be called in and he told Mr Noordam that he had a safe address for him. Mr Noordam, however, decided not to leave his boys. He had been called in to the SD headquarters on several occasions before and he had always got off with a warning. He was sure it would be the same this time too. But he was wrong. This time it was different.

On 8 September the SS came back to the area just at the end of the night's curfew. They set Van der Hoop's house on fire and then went to the home of Chris Blom. They asked his wife where he was. When she said that she had no idea they threatened to smash up everything in the house. Mrs Blom, however, remained calm and replied: 'You do what you like, my children and I are going on with our breakfast.' Her attitude commanded respect, and after searching the house they left, convinced that she really did not know the whereabouts of her husband. They told her, however, that they would find him in the end and that they had reserved a bullet for him.

Another group of the SS went to Valkenheide. Everybody was told to go to the chapel. Mr Noordam was ill in bed. He was ordered to get dressed, was sat on a chair on his doorstep and summarily shot. Several members of the staff were badly beaten, and hand-grenades were thrown into the house of one of the staff. He had a Jewish girl hidden in an attic room. She, of course, had not gone to the chapel with the others. Suddenly the ceiling came down and she was surrounded by debris. It was a miracle that she was neither killed nor discovered.

When Mr Noordam was buried in the ground of Valkenheide, only his family and the staff were allowed to attend the funeral. None of the boys who had loved him so much was allowed to pay his respects. Neither were any of the villagers permitted to attend. After the war the SS officer responsible denied ever having given his word of honour to Mrs Van der Hoop that nobody would be harmed.

In Wijk bij Duurstede the consequences of the arrests of the two Nazis were terrible. One member of the Resistance managed to flee in a nun's habit to a local convent. In those days the rules in convents were very strict and no man, apart from priests and doctors, was allowed to go anywhere but the visitors' room, let alone stay overnight. In this case the Archbishop of Utrecht gave special dispensation and the diver stayed in the convent for several months.

Furious that they could not find the members of the Resistance they must have identified and were looking for in Wijk bij Duurstede, the Germans ransacked and looted their houses. The three sons of the farmer who had helped the Resistance with their prisoners, Mr Van Laar, had decided to go into hiding too, as they felt vulnerable in the midst of all this German activity in the area, even though they were not members of the Resistance and were classified as farm workers. On this morning they had returned to the farm to finish some necessary work. They kept a look-out on the road from Wijk, planning to run off if they saw a German car. However, the

Germans approached from the Amerongen road and the brothers failed to see them in time. Two of them, Willem and Gert, tried to run and the Germans shot them while their father watched, horrified, unable to do anything. The third son stood still where he was. He was arrested and sent to a concentration camp. He did survive the war but his father never recovered from that awful tragedy. It was all the worse because the Van Laar brothers had had nothing to do with the whole affair of the abduction of the burgemeester and his friend.

Van der Hoop joined a Resistance group in another part of the country. He was arrested in February 1945 and later executed. His wife was allowed to go home after a few weeks in detention. When she arrived at her house there was nothing left but blackened rubble.

In other towns, similar arrests of Nazis were made at this time but nowhere else were there any reprisals. Only where the SS were present was there great brutality and senseless killing.

Sabotage on the roads

At the beginning of September the commander of the Utrecht region of the Resistance ordered that no more German traffic should be allowed to go through his area. Later on it turned out that he was acting on information from the Allies about what they wanted the local Resistance to do. This area was, of course, very important for the movement of German troops towards Arnhem, although we did not know about the planned Allied air drop there.

The best way to stop a German car or lorry was either to block the road or to see to it that the vehicle's tyres were punctured. Roads could be blocked only well away from towns and villages, as that kind of job took too long to go unnoticed. In Leersum a Resistance group went out one night to fell two beech trees on the road to Amerongen. When a large tree is felled it makes a loud noise as it comes down; to avoid attracting attention twice, the trees had therefore to be toppled simultaneously. This took careful planning. Two men worked on each tree. It was a difficult job as the diameter of the trunk was larger than the length of the bow-saw. The men had to work with the equipment they had or could safely borrow; it was no longer possible to buy a suitable saw. The sawing had to be done with circular movements and was exhausting work. One man had the best job: he kept a look-out on the road. Another synchronised the operation: he went from one pair of sawers to the other to make sure that they would both be ready at the same time. Eventually the trees could be sawn through, in such a way that they would fall across the road, one from each side. You can still see today that the beautiful line of beeches on that road is interrupted in two places.

To give the Germans flat tyres a blacksmith invented a device made of two nails, which he bent so that each nail formed a right angle. He snipped off the heads and sharpened them so that each nail had two points. The nails were intertwined and welded together at the angles. Whichever way they were thrown in the road they had a spike pointing upwards. The BS called them 'Hunheads' and they were very effective. I took bags full of these nails round my district and distributed them. In the evening and through the night it was wonderfully satisfying to hear the German cars blow their tyres and stop. Sometimes the Germans forced Dutch civilians to help mend the punctures, but even that did not spoil our sense of achievement and feeling of satisfaction.

Of course the Germans retaliated. On 7 September they put up a poster which said: 'Every household is responsible for seeing to it that the road outside their property is free of nails and that there is nothing in the road that can cause a German vehicle to have a puncture. Should any such object be discovered in the road, then the oldest member of the family in front of whose house the object is found will be arrested. Anyone in possession of a nail will be executed on the spot.' Another poster announced that for every act of sabotage five hostages would be taken and executed immediately.

On 12 September, as a reprisal for the sabotage on the roads, the Germans decided to burn down a house. They left the choice to a local Nazi, who selected the house belonging to burgemeester Van den Bosch of Leersum. He had long since been sacked by the Germans and replaced by a member of the Nazi Party. To all the local inhabitants, however, he still remained 'the burgemeester'. When the Germans arrived at the house they asked for the owner, but fortunately he was not at home, otherwise he might have been arrested. The family were ordered out of the house. They were allowed to take their papers, ration cards and some clothes, but nothing else: no family heirlooms, no furniture, no food, no paintings. While the family stood outside, the Germans threw chairs on top of the tables, then poured petrol over the furniture and set it alight. All the windows were smashed with bayonets in order to fan the flames. There was nothing anyone could do.

Jan Lagemaat turned out with the fire brigade. The Germans let them run out the hoses but forbade them to turn on the taps. Only when there was nothing left but some smouldering debris was the fire brigade allowed to put this out. The family had kept their food in the cellar. The Germans took it all away and had a big dinner party, using the stolen food. Everyone who witnessed this exhibition of wanton vandalism felt extremely angry, as well as frustrated and helpless. How we detested these Nazis and wanted them out of the country. Friends took in the family. The burgemeester became a diver and stayed outside the village. His daughter Ila (code-name Annie), who was the courier for the Leersum section of the BS, stayed with friends and was able to carry on with her work, more determined than ever.

The Resistance is busy
On 17 September the Dutch Government-in-exile gave orders for a general railway strike. As nearly all the railway workers obeyed, no more trains ran. The Germans now had to look after their own trains. One consequence was that all railway personnel had to go into hiding, as the Germans had of course forbidden the strike. This meant there was suddenly a lot of extra work for the LO, finding safe homes for thousands of them. Another consequence was that the Resistance couriers could no longer travel by train. Buses and trams were not running either, so mail could not be moved from one town to another, and there were no telephones we could use. From then on, all communications between members of the Resistance who lived any distance away were effected by couriers on bicycles. We girls were kept extremely busy and often had very long rides.

In the early days of the BS it was very difficult to obtain weapons, but later on the Allies dropped weapons for the Resistance. The first arms drop was carried out on 28 August 1944, but it took some time before all the groups were armed. Until then we had to make do, sometimes with defective guns. These could be useful in a situation where just threatening with a gun was sufficient.

In Doorn the group had a rifle that lacked a bolt. Their courier, Jantje Laporte, was an enterprising girl who always found a solution, however complicated the problem. This time she just walked into the hotel which had been requisitioned by the Germans. She coolly entered the guardroom while the guards were having their lunch and took the bolt out of one of the rifles that had been left there. The Germans would never have expected anyone to dare enter their domain, so the rifles were not guarded. Nevertheless Jantje could not have been sure of this, so it must have taken nerves of steel to walk in and out again like that. Jantje survived the war and now lives abroad.

43

As the possession of a weapon automatically carried the death penalty, it was essential to have a good hiding-place. The best place was in the woods, but then the guns had to be fetched every time they were needed. Sometimes arms were kept on a farm, where buildings usually had many hiding-places. When there was any danger of a German raid (the number of which tended to increase if the Germans were already active in the area) and our men could not go out, it was up to the girls to take the weapons to the different groups who needed them.

Sometimes sudden improvisation was necessary. I had gone in August 1944 to stay with the De Jong family in Langbroek. I slept in their attic. Gerrit de Jong was a hairdresser and also the local tobacconist, although by that time there was hardly any tobacco available and a coupon for a ration of it was rarely issued. Langbroek was such a small village, with only about 1,500 inhabitants, that there was no local Wehrmacht commander stationed there. There were also many minor roads and tracks where the Germans did not go: in fact it was a relatively good place for a girl in the Resistance to stay.

When the Langbroek Resistance group was to receive our share of the weapons and explosives we decided to hide them on one of the farms. Unfortunately arrangements for storing them there had not been completed when I arrived in the village with, among other things, a suitcase containing thirty hand-grenades. I was rather nervous about bumping along on my bicycle with this particular load on my luggage rack, so I had taken the precaution of removing the detonators before I set off and had put them in my pockets. I went immediately to my local contact, Kees ten Wolde, the local school headmaster. There I reassembled the grenades. As there was no immediate safe storage available, the headmaster put the grenades and other items in a cupboard in his school. This seemed dangerous, because one of the children might innocently open the cupboard, which could not be locked. The best thing the headmaster could think of on the spur of the moment was to tell the parents that he had to close the school as there was a suspected case of diphtheria in the neighbourhood.

In 1944–5 there was a diphtheria epidemic. More than 100,000 people were afflicted and over 7,500 died of this illness. As there was no public transport, school inspectors did not visit the schools any more, so the chances of our secret and the headmaster's deception being found out were minimal. Since people were not immunised then as they are today, everyone was nervous about coming into contact with diphtheria and would keep away. If a case was suspected, a throat swab would be taken and someone had to cycle to the nearest laboratory, in this case 25 km (15 miles) away. A week later someone had to cycle to the laboratory for the results. It was the only way, as no letter could be posted to the doctor and no telephone call could be made.

The headmaster now had at least a week to find storage for these weapons. As soon as he had moved them safely out of the way, he informed the parents that the case had proved not to be diphtheria but an ordinary throat infection, which meant that the school would be open again. In the meantime Harry Hello and Joop Alberts took the weapons and hid them, well wrapped up, under some branches in a ditch in an orchard.

The arrangements almost went wrong at the last moment. Harry and Joop had loaded everything, together with some Sten guns which had also arrived, on to a handcart – there was too much to be carried on a bicycle. While they were pushing the cart, a German appeared on a bicycle. Some German soldiers did try to make friends with the Dutch, and this fellow was apparently one of those. He kindly offered to help push, but Harry and Joop told him they could manage. He never asked what their load consisted of. Sometimes we were very lucky indeed.

3

Secret Services

Introduction

My part in this work was limited to the carrying and collation of information gathered by other people. This was tiring and dangerous enough. Yet the story of those who set up and operated intelligence networks, in particular the brave agents, radio operators, householders and farmers who let them use their buildings, all of whom were exposed to huge risks and many of whom paid with their lives, is very central to the story of the Resistance in my area – as, indeed, it was elsewhere.

Before the war started, the British Secret Intelligence Service (SIS) had officers in the Netherlands who officially worked in the passport control office of the British Embassy in The Hague. When the Germans invaded the country the SIS officers just escaped at the last minute. Nobody stayed behind, and they did not leave any of their equipment. It would have been useful if either the British or Dutch Governments had left some radio transmitters and instructions about their use with trustworthy people, but no one apparently had the foresight to make arrangements for such contingency plans. When they had to evacuate, events moved so fast that there was no time for anyone to discuss it. Consequently the Resistance had to do the best they could and make their own radio links with Britain and organise routes for a courier service via Switzerland or Sweden. Several separate intelligence services were active throughout the war. For example, the OD had a service organised by a Dutch officer, J. M. Somer, before he escaped to England in 1942. In London the Dutch Government-in-exile founded the Bureau Inlichtingen (BI), or Intelligence Bureau, and put Somer in charge. Dutchmen who had managed to escape to England were trained as secret agents and were then flown back and parachuted into the Netherlands. Herman

Leus, alias Jacques, and Jan de Bloois, known as Piet de Springer, who worked in Langbroek, belonged to this organisation.

The Geheime Dienst Nederland (GDN) was another Dutch intelligence organisation founded and run by the Resistance. This gathered together German military data and also political and economic information which was sent to the BI in London. Towards the end of the war information was also sent to the south of the Netherlands, which was liberated before the rest of the country.

The Raad van Verzet (RVV) had wireless operators, among whom we had three in Langbroek at the same time. (It was remarkable that the Germans failed to pinpoint any of the transmitting stations or detect the men involved.) These operators were Wiebe (A. Stanthardt), Gerrit (Schotanus), and Dick Last. The LO (Assistance to Divers) and the LKP (action groups) had their own intelligence service, called Centrale Inlichtingen Dienst or CID.

In addition, M.I.9, British Military Intelligence, sent in Dick Kragt (also known as Captain Kay) in June 1943, with orders to set up an escape route via Maastricht to Belgium. He was very unlucky because instead of being dropped in the prearranged place he landed quite a long way away, just missing a church steeple and bumping heavily into a tree. Worse, he lost all his equipment, which was found soon afterwards by the Germans, so they knew the next day that there was an agent in the vicinity. Dick was able to contact the Resistance, but without a wireless set life became complicated. He had to use a Dutch contact to transmit his messages until another wireless operator was assigned to him some time later. Moreover, he would have been found out the first time his papers were checked, because the identity card which M.I.9 had given him was a very poor forgery. The Resistance had to find him more convincing papers! The Special Air Service (SAS) also sent in agents, among them Gilbert Sadi Kirschen, whose code-name was Captain King. He worked near Maarn.

Arrests and executions
The hills to the east of Utrecht were ideal for harbouring secret agents and operating secret transmitters. There were big stretches of forest and heathland, and an agent could hide a transmitter well away from any buildings. It was relatively easy to cycle from one town or village to another without using main roads. There were also open areas with scattered farms, where you could see Germans from a long way off if they decided to come your way.

The equipment the agents had at that time was very primitive – heavy and cumbersome – compared with what is in use today. The wireless operator also needed to use a very long aerial, which had to be put up outside.

The best location for a signal station was a lonely house or farm, as otherwise in a town or village the neighbours might wonder why a couple of times a day they could see a piece of wire sticking out of a window. Houses had to be found where the owners did not scare easily. Having a secret transmitter in your home automatically carried the death penalty if it was discovered.

The RVV wanted a radio station in the neighbourhood of Maarn. A complete station consisted of four or six signal stations at a distance of 3–4 km (1.8–2.4 miles) apart. These were used in irregular order to make it difficult for the Germans to take bearings.

The RVV found what they thought was the ideal house, from the point of view of its position, in Doorn. 'Le Chalet' was situated on the outskirts of the town, with a forest opposite. A long drive led up to the house, which had a large garden and this in turn was surrounded by woods. You could not even see the house from the road. They gave this station the code-name of 'The Goat's Stable', because the family kept a goat.

Mrs Van der Aa and her daughter Jacky, a bright, vivacious girl with brown, curly hair, in her early twenties, lived at Le Chalet. Jacky had a flair for making clothes. Even in wartime she could conjure up an evening dress out of a curtain and look terrific in it. What the RVV did not know – and Jacky said nothing about it, as she had been warned never to speak of it – was that because she was very good at drawing and painting she worked for one of the other secret services, forging identity cards. The family also had a Jewish diver living with them. An RVV member told me after the war that if the RVV had known these things they would not have increased the risk by using the Van der Aas' house.

So it was that in the evenings, before curfew, the wireless operator Ab van de Kerkhof would arrive to transmit his messages during the night from a barn behind the house. Mrs Van der Aa, who was a very caring person, would make sandwiches for him to eat while he was working. Perhaps if he had not been so well fed there he would not have come to the house so often.

One bright, clear night at the beginning of June 1944 when he was transmitting, Ab noticed a plane which seemed to be circling the house. He wondered if the Germans could take bearings from an aircraft, and he reported it. With hindsight it seems that the leaders of this operation were very naïve, because, instead of withdrawing the operator from this location to be on the safe side, they decided on 2 June 1944 that next time they would send a second operator to Le Chalet to help keep watch. But of course they had no means of telling how the German intelligence service itself conducted its business. To compound the ensuing disaster, it was the leader of the RVV's radio service, Th. W. la Rivière, an electrical engineer, who went as the extra man.

Mrs Van der Aa had a fox-terrier who always barked if a stranger came anywhere near the house. On 11 June the dog was found dead. The vet who came diagnosed poisoning. Even then it never seemed to have occurred to anyone that it might have been done deliberately to prevent the dog from warning the family of a raid.

In those days the Germans went round in vans with equipment to detect illegal radio transmissions. Looking back on this episode, it seems likely that too many transmissions were made from the Goat's Stable and that this is how they were discovered – for there was never any evidence elsewhere of detection from the air. We shall never know.

Not even the date, 13 June, stopped Ab from transmitting, soon after midnight. He could not hear anything from outside as he was wearing headphones. La Rivière was keeping watch from inside the barn, but it did not make any difference. The Germans came unnoticed up the drive to the house with three cars full of soldiers. Everyone was arrested: Mrs Van der Aa, Jacky, both wireless operators and the Jewish diver. None of them would survive the war. It was a complete disaster.

Mrs Van der Aa and Jacky were sent to Vught concentration camp. They were accused, first, of sheltering a Jew. Of course, they both denied knowing he was Jewish. Second, they were accused of giving agents the opportunity to use their barn for transmissions to the enemy. As the operators had been caught in the act they could not deny this.

Mother and daughter were interrogated separately and not allowed to meet, so that they could not compare notes. On 6 September, the day after 'Mad Tuesday', both were included in the transfer of women prisoners to Ravensbrück which took place then. A survivor from this camp told the family after the war that in August the inmates of Vught had heard news of the Allied advance and had been convinced that liberation was near. Instead, they had travelled for three days and nights, with seventy to eighty women packed into each goods van. They had kept up their courage by singing national songs.

In Ravensbrück conditions were atrocious. Every morning they had to stand for three hours in icy cold for the roll-call. They received very little food and had to work hard in the Siemens factory, where spare parts for aeroplanes were being manufactured. Many fellow prisoners wrote after the war that the Van der Aas had been so courageous, always cheering others up and helping them. Jacky never lost her creativity. On the red handkerchief which she had been given by the Red Cross in Vught she embroidered with white thread all sorts of sayings, and symbols such as a barred window, and the first lines of hymns that the prisoners used to sing.

Typhoid fever was going round Ravensbrück, as were other diseases. Mrs Van der Aa fell victim to typhoid. Even when her mother was dying, Jacky was not allowed to visit her and she did not hear of her death until several days later. Her mother had been in another hut and it took some time for friends to get the message through. Jacky became very weak through lack of food and she also died, not long after her mother.

Ab van de Kerkhof was executed in Vught and La Rivière was sent to a German concentration camp, from which he did not return. Nobody ever found out what happened to the Jewish diver. It is most likely that he died in Auschwitz.

On 14 August 1944 an arrest was made in Driebergen. Albert van der Heyden was a textile engineer who had travelled extensively before the war to Belgium and France. He was allowed to continue with his business, but apart from his normal work he also took microfilms with him to Brussels and Paris. From France they went via Switzerland to Britain. Albert worked for the OD secret service department. He also took escaping RAF pilots to the south of the Netherlands and passed them on to a bargeman, who hid them in his boat and took them over to Belgium.

The Van der Heyden family had a Jewish child staying with them. Fortunately the little girl had just left to spend a few days with another family as a kind of holiday. Her parents had been arrested and sent to Westerbork. They had written to their daughter and when the Germans searched the house this letter was found.

'Helping Jews as well!' the German officer in charge of the arrest shouted furiously. So they had obviously found out about some of Albert's other activities.

Albert was taken to Vught. No one knows for certain what happened to him. The Red Cross told the family that he was executed with the others who were killed round 'Mad Tuesday'. His death was not officially recorded, however, and some ex-prisoners said after the war that they had seen him in a German concentration camp. To this day the family does not know what became of him.

Agents in Langbroek

Jan de Bloois was a farmer's son, and he lived near Rotterdam. On 8 October 1943 he escaped with eleven other young men in a small boat. They left the Dutch coast at 11.30 p.m. and at 4 a.m. the motor gave out. The boat drifted helplessly in the North Sea for three hours, until at last a mechanic on board managed to restart the engine. At 4.30 p.m. they were spotted by HMS *Campbell*, who picked them up. By a lucky chance one of the officers on board turned out to be a friend of one of the escapers. The men had a marvellous time while HMS *Campbell* continued to patrol the North Sea. In the evening they broadcast the message that Jan had told his family to listen for: 'Hear, see and keep silence.' His parents now knew that he had arrived safely in England. Jan became attached to BI and was trained as a secret agent, taking the name of Piet de Springer, because he would have to jump from an aeroplane to return to the Netherlands.

Piet was tall and fair-haired and an outdoor type. He was quiet and reserved – good qualities for an agent – and he had a strong will. Never one to give up if he wanted something done, he would just say, 'It has got to be done' – and it was. On the night of 7–8 May 1944 he parachuted down in the Province of Noord-Brabant. His task was to work as a liaison officer and decoder for the RVV, which had had a radio link with Britain for about a year then. Piet brought with him four radios, but he landed so heavily that they were all broken. He had been given strict orders not to get in touch with his family. One day he had to visit a house not far from his old home, and by chance his grandmother saw him cycling past, but Piet gave no sign of recognition.

In September 1944 the RVV sent Piet to a contact man in Wijk bij Duurstede. They met in a pub and Piet said, as instructed, 'I have come to pay the bill,' and he put five Dutch coins on the table so that they made the letter V. Then the contact man took Piet to Langbroek.

Piet had acquired some wirelesses to replace the damaged ones. His main concern at that moment was to see to it that there was a radio link from that area to Britain. Around Langbroek there were three suitable farms. These were the Jacobshoeve on the Gooyerdijk in Leersum, owned by farmer Kobus van Doorn; the family where Kees Swaluwenburg lived on the Langbroekerdijk; and the chicken farm on the Cotherweg, owned by Jeanne van Kleef.

The Van Kleef house was 240 metres (almost 265 yards) from the main road, so no one could see an aerial stuck out of a window. Jeanne was already a member of the local Resistance group and she knew how to keep her own counsel. The Resistance called her house 'The Silent Front'. She lived with her aged father and her brother, whose work on the farm gave him exemption from having to work for the Germans. From September to December 1944 two secret agents and four radio operators were active in and around Langbroek, in addition to the Langbroek Resistance group and me.

The other agent, Herman Leus, or 'Jacques', was a friend of Piet; they had trained together. Jacques had walked most of the way from the Netherlands to Portugal. It had taken him almost a year. He had crossed the Pyrenees on foot, which had been particularly hazardous, but in the end he had made it. In April 1944 he took a quicker route back to the Netherlands by parachuting into the south of the country, where he trained a member of the Resistance, Corneille du Corbier, code-named Kees, as a wireless operator and took him to the Swaluwenburgs' farm in Langbroek.

It was Piet de Springer who had arranged for wireless operators to work from the farm. He had become friendly with the Swaluwenburgs – Mrs Swaluwenburg made him his favourite pancakes for his birthday. He had been very honest with the family about the risks. 'If we are caught,' he told the farmer, 'they will put us all up against the wall.' Farmer Swaluwenburg decided that there was more to being a good citizen then wearing an orange ribbon on the Queen's birthday, and he consented.

Some five months later, on 23 September, Jacques and Kees received orders to leave for Ermelo on the Veluwe, to set up a radio link there. The Veluwe is an area north of Arnhem that stretches to the IJsselmeer. Nowadays there is reclaimed land between the Veluwe and the IJsselmeer, but at the time the name referred to what was largely woods and heathland. The RVV sent Dick Last to the Swaluwenburgs as a replacement.

Dick had been a wireless operator in the Dutch Merchant Navy before the war. His radio link now functioned for a hundred days. He was in contact with London and the liberated south of the

MI9 agent Captain Kay
Dick Kragt

Jacky van der Aa, 1920–1945

B.E. van der Aa-Meertens,
1893–1945

Piet de Springer
Jan de Bloois, 1916–1944

Above:
Cornelis Swaluwenburg, 1884-1964

Above right:
Johanna Swaluwenburg-Van Leeuwen, 1886-1964

SAS agent Captain King
Gilbert Sadi Kirschen

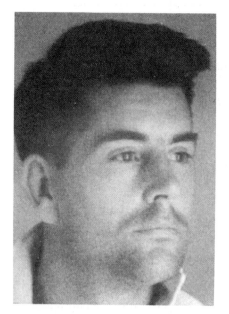

Dick Last

Roelof van Valkenburg,
1917-1990

Netherlands twice a day during this time, which can be considered a record. He stayed with the Swaluwenburgs, acting as a farm labourer. It was a problem that the Germans in that area liked to go shooting for pheasants and rabbits, which of course Dutch people were not allowed to do. At any moment soldiers could walk into the farm, demanding a glass of milk or wanting to know what the farmer was doing.

If it did not seem safe to use the radio, Dick would put his set on the luggage rack of his bicycle and cycle to the Jacobshoeve farm in Leersum to work from there. Eventually the Germans requisitioned the whole of the Swaluwenburgs' farm. They decided the family could just as well live with the cows during the day, and they allowed them into the house only at night to sleep. Dick then had to make all his radio contacts from the Jacobshoeve farm.

After Jacques and Kees left, two other radio operators, Wiebe and Gerrit, came to Langbroek. Like Dick, Wiebe had been a wireless operator in the Merchant Navy and Gerrit had done a similar job in the Dutch Royal Navy. They stayed with Jeanne van Kleef and had daily radio contact with both Britain and the liberated south. This meant that between September and the end of December 1944 very heavy radio traffic with the Allies took place around Langbroek.

The Germans were often out with their detector vans driving slowly through the towns and villages while they took bearings, which is why the radio operator's job was so dangerous. When the German vans were not in use they were kept at Lunenburg Castle, one of some dozen castles in the Langbroek area. It happened that there was no Roman Catholic church in the village, there being few Catholics in that part of the country, and on Sundays a priest would come from a neighbouring village to conduct Mass in one of the outbuildings of the castle.

On a Sunday morning in November 1944, while Mass was being said, the castle was bombed, probably because of the many German vehicles thought to be stationed there. One woman was killed, and she happened to be the sister-in-law of Kees Swaluwenburg. This caused some bad feeling in the family, as Kees had harboured all those agents who had apparently reported where a bomb or two could put many German vehicles out of action. This was yet another example of the dangers faced by the general population, while the Allies tried to weaken the Germans by attacks from the air. The loss of life on this occasion was particularly sickening because the Germans had moved their cars out of the castle only days before the raid.

An SAS agent

Twice a day Piet de Springer took the incoming radio messages to RVV Post 4, which was an open space in the Maarn forest. From there the messages went to Gilbert Sadi Kirschen (Captain King), a Belgian lawyer who had reached Britain in 1940 by way of Spain and Portugal to join the SAS. He had earlier worked with the Maquis in France and had been imprisoned there but managed to escape.

On the night of 14–15 September 1944 he had parachuted into the Netherlands with two wireless operators. They had made a perfect drop, with all the equipment undamaged. The RVV had had a reception committee ready to meet him with the agreed flashlight code. The next day Kirschen met the chief of the RVV, a man nicknamed Lange Jan, or Long John, because of his height. Lange Jan introduced Kirschen to Roelof van Valkenburg, who became his liaison officer. Roelof was a medical student whose studies were interrupted by the war. His fiancée, Bep Labouchère, became the courier.

Kirschen was very security-conscious. He allowed no one but Roelof and Bep to know where he was. His mission was to find out about German troop movements in the area, the locations of the V-2 rockets, which were greatly worrying the British at that time, what kind of fuel these rockets used, and what targets should be bombed. He thought this job would take less than a week, but in the end he had to stay for six months. The airborne landings at Arnhem took place two days after he arrived, and it became clear why he had been sent to this particular area. Unfortunately the Allies lost the battle of Arnhem and Kirschen had to stay where he was.

He moved frequently, for security reasons, but did manage to stay for three months at one address, the home of Vera Hoogeweegen. She lived with her ten-year-old son in a large house in the Maarn forest. At the beginning of 1944 it was used as a radio station. Lange Jan also went to stay there and her house became the headquarters of the RVV. In addition to working with Roelof and Bep, Kirschen also worked with a Resistance group led by a man known as Maarten, who also belonged to the RVV.

Maarten's group

Maarten's courier was Cathrien, one of Bep's sisters. The group varied according to the kind of job that had to be done. One of Maarten's tasks was to seek out suitable dropping fields, so that the Allies could send in radios, arms and material for sabotage. It was not easy to find such spaces because the specifications were very precise: they had to be 500 metres (550 yards) long and 300–400 metres (330–440 yards) wide; at least 10 km (6 miles) from large built-up areas and from searchlights; at least 15 km (9 miles) from German flak; and 3 km (1.8 miles) from German sentries.

When the dropping zone had been approved it was given a code-name and a code-sentence. A group of twelve to fifteen men were needed as a reception committee because the containers of weapons were very heavy and had to be moved quickly once they had landed. It was very likely that the Germans would hear a plane approach and turn back, and that they would start a search. All parachutes had to be buried speedily and no tell-tale signs could be left. The phase of the moon was very important too. The night could not be so light that doing a job like this during curfew hours would be too risky, but it could not be so dark that you could not see the parachutes coming down and might either fail to locate the precious cargo or be struck by a container and killed.

The Resistance listened to the Belgian news broadcast in the afternoon to learn when a drop would be made. If after the news the code-sentence for your dropping zone was read out, the reception committee had to be on standby. If the code-sentence was repeated in the evening, at the end of the Radio Orange broadcast, it meant that the drop was on. The Germans were unable to make head or tail of the coded messages. The announcer would say: 'Aunt Marie has a birthday' or 'Uncle Lewis's horse has died' and the group who had been given those code-sentences knew what they had to do that night.

As soon as they heard the plane, the committee members would briefly light up the corners of the dropping zone and one person would give the agreed letter in Morse code by means of a flashlight. Sometimes, however, things would go wrong. For example, if the plane crew was even one minute late in throwing the containers out, the plane would travel so far that the dropping area would be missed.

Maarten once had his containers coming down several miles away. It was impossible to find them in the dark as they could have landed anywhere. In fact he heard the next day that the Germans had found everything, so not only had he lost the supplies but the Germans now knew that a group was being armed in the area.

On another occasion Maarten, Roelof, Cathrien and another member, Jan van Dijk, returned during the day to unpack containers they had hidden in an empty house during the night. By chance two Germans were looking for divers at a nearby address and they came to this house too. Maarten and Roelof were arrested, as they were unable to get away, but luckily the others managed to escape through the back door. One German left to fetch reinforcements while the other kept his rifle pointing at the two men, who had to stand there with their hands up. When the German momentarily took his eye off them Roelof made the gesture of pulling a trigger with his index finger. Cathrien, who by now had worked her way round to the front and was standing outside, pretending to be a hiker adjusting her pack, saw this through the window and signalled to Jan van Dijk, who was hiding behind some shrubs. Jan crept up and shot the German in the leg which enabled them all to escape. Again, of course, they lost their containers.

Gathering intelligence
Using all the radios, these various operators sent messages about German troop movements and the units involved, the building of defence works or anything unusual that had happened. Along all the main roads members of the Resistance were making notes about any German traffic that passed their houses. It might be a report of a single German on a bicycle or of a long column of soldiers. As far as possible the badges and numbers on vehicles, or anything which might help to identify the unit, were recorded. When we compared the counts on all sides of crossroads, we could work out the direction of troop movements. As there was no public transport and the Dutch were not allowed cars, all vehicular traffic was down to the Germans.

It was a long, tedious job, sitting for hours at a window overlooking a main road and keeping your eye on what travelled past. In many Dutch houses the windows are large, and it is easy to see inside. To pull the curtains across in daytime would have drawn attention to the house, so soon the women who mostly carried out this watch on the traffic were called 'the knitting ladies'. A woman sitting by her window with knitting in her hands did not look as suspicious as a man would have done. At night, of course, men could watch too, from darkened rooms. Reports from Doorn were important, as from there one road went to Utrecht and one to Amersfoort.

I had to cycle twice a day from Veenendaal, where at that time the headquarters of my Resistance group was, through the towns and villages along the Utrecht chain of hills, a distance of 45 km (27 miles), to collect all the information the watchers had gathered. When I was back in Veenendaal I helped to compare the different reports and then made a summary. I took this to a contact address in Scherpenzeel, some 12 km (7 miles) away, where it was collected by Kirschen's courier, Bep, so that he could send the details over his radio.

I worked a long day. I left at 6 a.m., as soon as the curfew ended, to collect the night's reports, and I set off again on the afternoon round at 3 p.m. During the battle of Arnhem the Resistance had made telephone links between towns in the battle zone, which worked from the power station of the electricity company in Arnhem. One connection worked between Bennekom and Nijmegen. This meant that I had to make a trip to Bennekom too (some 10 km/ 6 miles east of Veenendaal), in order to take the reports of German traffic there to be phoned to Nijmegen. I did this between the early morning and the afternoon runs. Altogether this amounted to 135 km (80 miles) a day, seven days a week, which was exhausting on the small amount of food we had. When, towards the winter, the front came to a standstill, these trips round the towns were scaled down to one a day.

The GDN also logged the German traffic. They made topographical sketches, too, of German headquarters and bunkers, both fake and real ones. This was very dangerous work as it is practically impossible to make a good map without taking notes near the site. All maps and sketches drawn by the GDN were kept and it is amazing to see how detailed they are. On 10 September the German Field Marshal Model set up his headquarters in a large manor house in Doorn. Kathy Kuylaars, who was a regional scout for the GDN, made a report with a detailed map which was sent to the Allies on the same day. Unfortunately the field marshal stayed there for only two nights before leaving for Oosterbeek. Here he was surprised a few days later by the airborne attack on Arnhem.

In Driebergen the Germans built a bunker which they camouflaged as a large two-storey house. The walls were painted the colour of bricks and lines were drawn on them so that they really looked like bricks. Several dummy windows were also painted on the front of the 'house'. The GDN reported this, accompanied by a map.

There were now several organisations doing the same thing. This was not wasteful, however, because not every radio always worked. Sometimes suddenly an operator could not use his radio because Germans had arrived too close to the signal station for safety, so it was useful if several people were trying to transmit the same information. It also added weight to a report if several agents thought it important enough to pass on.

4
Helping Allied Escapers

Introduction

The flight paths of RAF and USAAF aircraft on their way to and from Germany regularly went over the Netherlands, so many British and American planes were shot down over my country. Aircrew members who landed safely had to try to evade the enemy. The Resistance organised escape lines to help them to return to their bases.

Before this, in 1940, about a thousand members of the Belgian and French armed forces had managed to escape imprisonment in Germany. They crossed our frontier and looked to us for help in reaching Belgium. Because of this early involvement with escapers, many Dutch families had made contact with one another as they passed men on to friends or friends of friends they could trust. These contacts were used again when it became necessary to find safe houses for escaping Allied airmen.

Many people who hid an airman did not, in those days, speak English, but the word 'pilot' sounds similar to the Dutch 'piloot', so they recognised it. Before long navigators, rear gunners and other aircrew found it was easier to call themselves 'pilots' too, as did many of the stranded soldiers of the Airborne Division who fought at Arnhem later.

It was vital to return as many aircrew as possible to Britain, not only because the Allies could not afford to lose trained men but also because it was good for morale. The airmen knew that they had a fair chance of returning home if they survived being shot down.

A Dutch organisation called 'Fiat Libertas' started early on in the war to help escaping aircrew. Not only was it a risky business to travel with someone who looked different from the local people, did not speak the language and was obviously of military age, but also the Germans tried to infiltrate their spies into the escape system, disguised as British airmen, so that they could discover the safe houses along the line. Helping Allied escapers carried the death penalty and this was no idle threat. Five men in a suburb of Rotterdam who did no more than give sandwiches to a British aircrew who had had to make an emergency landing were executed.

So every man who claimed to belong to the Allies had to be vetted by someone who spoke English fluently. One of these was Mr J. D. Waller, the managing director of a factory in Utrecht, who lived in a large house in Driebergen. He had a list of questions, such as:

'What is a pancake?' (Landing with the undercarriage up.)
'What is a gong?' (A medal)

The RAF had a magazine with a serial story about Pilot Officer Prune. Mr Waller would say casually, 'What has Pilot Officer Prune been up to lately?' It was highly unlikely that a German would know the answer to that one, however well he could speak English.

During the final year of the war these screening precautions were no longer necessary; by then we had good radio links with Britain and name, rank and number could be checked immediately.

In the early years the airmen were taken to Belgium, usually as far as possible by train, with the guides travelling in a different compartment so that if something went wrong they could not be linked to their charges. If one stage of the journey could not be managed we had to wait until the all-clear was given, which meant that sometimes escapers had to stay for weeks on end with a family. Crossing the Dutch–Belgian border was easiest on foot. It was impossible for the Germans to guard every small path through the woods.

Mr Waller's luck ran out on 1 April 1944 when he was one of thirty-five members of 'Fiat Libertas' who were arrested. They were tried by a German military court in Utrecht. While the group was waiting in the hall of the court, Mr Waller passed the word along to the others that they should say he was a big man with fair hair. As he was short and dark, he told the Germans that they had the wrong man and he denied ever having been involved with Allied aircrews. In the end they gave him the benefit of the doubt, sentencing him to life imprisonment. Of the others, twenty-one received a death sentence. They were sent to Germany to be executed. For fourteen months they waited, expecting every day to be shot, but a bureaucratic mix-up saved their lives. Mr Waller was kept in eleven different prisons, in atrocious conditions. In one prison he received almost no food and had to share his single cell with twenty other prisoners.

He was liberated by the Americans in April 1945.

After Arnhem
Helping escapers was also one of Piet de Springer's tasks. After the Allies lost the battle of Arnhem and retreated during the night of 25–26 September 1944, many soldiers were stranded on the north bank of the Rhine. They were wandering about in the woods of the Veluwe or were trying to find farmers to take them in. A few of them managed to contact the Resistance and were taken to Langbroek. Piet de Springer rowed them across the Rhine at night to rejoin the Allies.

Leo Heaps, a Canadian officer, had been taken prisoner during the battle of Arnhem. On 26 September he and a British sergeant called Kettley were in a large group of POWs being taken to Germany. They both jumped from the train – which sounds a dangerous thing to do, but trains in those days did not go as fast as more modern ones, and trains to Germany had to go very slowly until they reached the border because the Resistance kept on sabotaging the railway lines.

Heaps and Kettley contacted the Resistance group which was working with the Belgian SAS agent Gilbert Sadi Kirschen (Captain King). They were lucky to have found them because Kirschen had a wireless operator who was in touch with the Allies twice a day. The bona fides of the two men could therefore be checked immediately. They were able to arrange for them to set off on 5 October for the already liberated southern part of the Netherlands. Bep Labouchère, Roelof van Valkenburg's fiancée, was their guide for the first part of the journey. She cycled ahead of them, looking out for German patrols and road-blocks, and took them to a rendezvous in the Maarn forest where Piet de Springer was waiting. She then returned home, while Piet took the two men to Langbroek, where Jeanne van Kleef gave them a meal at her farm and the opportunity for a much needed rest, as they were not as used to cycling as we Dutch were.

Later Piet took the soldiers to the Rhine. The north bank was out of bounds to the Dutch, but it was a long bank and between Amerongen and Wijk bij Duurstede the area was so thinly populated that there were stretches without German sentries. They could not guard every yard of the dyke. In any case, they probably never thought that people might try to cross the river at that particular spot.

In the daytime you could see a good distance ahead. If there were no sentries and no Germans had been spotted in the area, it was safe to row across the river. Piet kept a rowing-boat hidden in the reeds that grew along the bank. Heaps and Kettley were taken across to the village of Maurik, where another Resistance group took over and helped them to reach Tiel. From there another boatman took them across the River Waal. Once across that, they were in the liberated part of the country. The escape route established in this way looked very promising.

Heaps and Kettley suggested to M.I.9 that this route should be used to try to recover the stranded Airborne troops. The authorities, however, thought it would be better if the men were to cross the river nearer to Arnhem, which, if it could be done, would be easier, as most men were hiding in that area. On the night of 22–23 October, 138 Airborne men crossed the Rhine between Wageningen and Renkum, at a location about 20 km (12 miles) east of the spot used by Piet de Springer. British patrols were waiting on the south bank and everyone arrived safely. This crossing was called Pegasus I after the emblem of the British Airborne troops. A second attempt, called Pegasus II, on the night of 17–18 November, was a disaster, however, as the group of Airbornes and their guides ran into a German patrol. Only eight soldiers got across, many others were taken prisoner, and a few gave the patrol the slip, melting into the night to roam around again until the Resistance could collect them once more. The Dutch guides were badly beaten up and three of them were subsequently executed. One guide was so severely injured that he died a week later in captivity.

The lesson we learned was that it was too dangerous to move the escapers in large groups. In future the men would have to travel in groups of not more than five at a time. Besides, it was by now impossible to get near the Rhine anywhere east of Amerongen, which included the place of the Pegasus I crossing, since the Germans had evacuated all towns east of Elst and had declared the area between these towns and the river out of bounds to the Dutch.

So Piet de Springer took small groups by bicycle to 'Den Duinen', a house in some 1–2 hectares (3 acres) of sand-dunes situated a few minutes' walk to the river between Amerongen and Wijk bij Duurstede. From Langbroek and other villages in the area these groups cycled along narrow roads and footpaths until they came to the river. Kirschen radioed to the Allies the names and numbers of the soldiers who could soon be expected, and Piet or two local men – Coen (Esveld), in his twenties, and Chris Cornelisse, who was middle-aged – rowed them across. If there were more than six men the little boat had to go twice. When it was not possible to make two journeys because the moon had risen too much or there was a security alert, the men stayed on farms in Langbroek or in sheds in a neighbouring orchard.

If you go to the Rhine near Amerongen you will find it looks very different today. After the war a barrage was built, as well as an island for recreational purposes, but before that the water in the river flowed much more rapidly. Heavy rainfall in the autumn of 1944 made the river rise to an abnormal level. Not since 1864 had the water been so high. The water-meadows were inundated, which made the river much wider; and once the cold weather set in, ice floes made crossing in a small boat even more hazardous. It needed much skill to row a full boat. Coen and Chris made three or four trips a week.

Bicycles

Great care had to be taken to see that all the bicycles the escapers had ridden were returned to their owners, so that they could be used again and, of course, so that the Germans did not come upon a large number of them lying beside the river. Bicycles were very precious. New ones were unobtainable as they were not being manufactured, and neither were tyres or spare parts.

At any time a German could stop a cyclist and commandeer the bicycle. You couldn't do anything about it. Germans also put up roadblocks and took the bicycle of anyone who chanced to come along. This could happen so unexpectedly – especially round a bend or at the corner of a street. You could not see it and take evasive action. If the Germans saw you trying to turn round and ride off they would order you to stop, and if you didn't they were very likely to shoot you.

My friend Ank Prevo advised me to wear a nurse's uniform when I was cycling about on Resistance business. She was three years older than I was and I always found her a tower of strength. If ever I was depressed she would help me to see things from a different perspective. Nurses were allowed to have a bicycle permit, and with an identity card stating your profession, and a uniform to go with it, you had a fair chance of being able to talk your way through if you were stopped at a checkpoint. Ank produced a uniform for me: it was a navy-blue dress with a white apron, and there was a long navy-blue head-dress, rather like a nun's. She had made the apron out of a sheet and the head-dress from the lining of a worn-out coat. It looked terrific and most convincing. I talked over the idea of wearing it with George, my group leader.

George van Spronsen had been a sports master in The Hague

before he was called up in 1939. When in 1943 all former soldiers had to go to a POW camp, he became a diver and went to Veenendaal because his company had been billeted there, so he knew quite a few people in that area. He became the leader of an action group which I joined in August 1944. He agreed that I should wear the uniform when I had to take a big risk – for example, if I was carrying weapons or explosives or a transmitter, or if I expected to be out after curfew. I did not want to wear it every day as it might look suspicious if people saw the same nurse on the same road several times a day. It was not practical anyway on a daily basis because I could not have kept the one white apron clean enough. Time had to be allowed for washing and drying it. Also you often needed more protection against the cold – most of the girl couriers wore slacks.

One problem with this identity was that I was too young to be a nurse. The minimum age then was twenty-three, plus a year for the obstetrics certificate. Consequently I was made four years older on my forged identity card.

Many girls in the Resistance carried false permits describing themselves as district nurses or midwives (it would have been unfortunate if we had been called on to demonstrate these skills!), or their papers said that they worked for the Ministry of Food Supply. As the Germans wanted to steal our food they liked the organisation of its supply to be good, so they allowed people who worked for this Ministry to keep their cycles. The cycle permits were signed by the local Wehrmacht commander, but, of course, the Resistance obtained blank permits which they filled in when they needed them.

Bicycles were the only means of transport after the railways went on strike. The food shortage was becoming desperate, too, in the last winter of the war, and the only way to reach a farm to try to obtain some extra vegetables, dairy produce or meat was by bicycle. In our area we might have to travel 15–30 km (10–20 miles) and that was too far to walk, certainly on worn-out shoes which could not easily be replaced either. In the west of the country some people would cycle over 100 km (60 miles) looking for food.

If four escaping soldiers had to be taken to the river at least two guides were necessary, because each one had to take back two cycles. This itself was dangerous, as one man with two cycles would obviously look conspicuous. Piet had worked out a way to travel with three bicycles – but this was even more conspicuous, so he only did it if he was fairly sure there were no Germans about. He tied the handlebars of one bike to the parcel carrier at the back of his own cycle so that the front wheel of the second bike was off the ground; the rear wheel then followed the leading bike. The third one he guided with one hand while he steered his own with the other hand. I don't know what story he had ready if the Germans stopped him and wanted to know why he had three bicycles, but he would have been unlucky to be stopped in this remote area. It was a risk he had to take.

We were astonished to discover that many Allied soldiers could not ride a bike and we had to teach them how to before we could move them. Dutch children learn to ride a tricycle as soon as they can walk, and by the age of four they can ride a bicycle. In normal weather conditions – not snow and ice – it would be most unusual to see a Dutchman fall off his bicycle, and such an event would have aroused the suspicion of any German who happened to witness it. This was an extra problem we could have done without. Another was that the escapers did not look like Dutchmen: they looked too well fed and their boots were in too good condition.

In the winter of 1944–5 there was a lot of snow and cycling was difficult at times, even for the Dutch. The escapers found it very hard going. They had to remember to keep to the right side of the road, and they were warned not to talk during the journey in case someone overheard them speaking English. They promised faithfully but, when they fell off, of course they automatically swore in English!

Sometimes there was no time to teach them how to ride a bike. Piet once had to fetch two escapers from Utrecht. He took with him on this mission Dit Alberts, who was the sixteen-year-old sister of Joop Alberts (see chapter 2). After trying vainly to get the escapers balanced on bicycles and moving safely, they had to give up and carry them instead on the parcel racks of their own bikes. It was no joke for Dit, cycling 30 km (20 miles) carrying a hefty man on her rack. During the war we would often see two people on one cycle, but a Dutchman would never let a girl do the work. It would have been unheard of. So they had to travel on all kinds of country byways to avoid arousing suspicion. This made the trip rather longer and more difficult than it should have been.

Clothing and food
Another problem was that the escapers needed civilian clothes and after four years of war it was not easy to supply them, for there were no replacements. Some local men gave all they had apart from what they stood up in, and that was asking a lot. One family who had an

enormous wardrobe before the war very generously gave clothes for the escapers whenever called upon. In the end the husband had barely a suit left.

Clothes were also used for bartering. With the food shortage being as bad as it was, normal business was done in that way. A good suit could be exchanged for several bags of potatoes or other items, and if you were hungry you were only too pleased with your bargain. Fortunately there were a number of farms in the Amerongen and Langbroek area, so the food shortage was not as desperate there as it was in other parts of the country and in the bigger towns. Nevertheless it was important to send the escapers on their way as soon as possible. They had no ration cards or any food with them, and having several healthy young men as guests could be a headache if you had to rely on the official rations.

Resistance members were often able to obtain extra food through their contacts, so that a person who was willing to take in an escaper but could not feed him was given food by the organisation. Sometimes it was possible to find a farmer with a pig ready for slaughter. One day a family had obtained a side of pork and while they were rejoicing about this good fortune Germans arrived to search the house. What were they to do? Their ten-year-old daughter was ill with measles, so her mother pushed the meat into her bed, alongside her, as that seemed the safest place. The slippery thing was not a very pleasant companion for the child but the ruse worked. When the Germans entered the girl's bedroom and saw her face covered in spots they left as quickly as they could. Germans were always terribly scared of contagious diseases.

At the beginning of October 1944 the Germans started evacuating the people who were living in the Betuwe area, but on 3 December, before the evacuation was completed, they blew up the dyke on the Rhine near Elden and the whole of the Betuwe was flooded. People who were still there had to be moved; their cattle too. The Germans did not care about the people, but they did not want the cows to drown. So they put the cattle in flat-bottomed boats and took them to the highest place they could find, which was the church in Maurik. The Amerongen branch of the Dutch Red Cross sent some very old rowing-boats, which were the best they could obtain, to rescue the elderly and infirm, and after that they saved other people who were living in their attics, which were just above the water-line. It was a weird Christmas that year in Maurik: instead of carols coming from the church, the Red Cross workers who stayed in the pub next door could hear only the lowing of cattle all night. Joop Alberts, who was a Red Cross worker helping with the evacuation of the elderly as well as a Resistance member, reported that it was impossible to reach the liberated south from Maurik as there was a lot of fighting going on. The Germans and British had patrols out and both sides suffered heavy losses.

A safe house in Maarn

On 29 January 1945 Coen made one more attempt to find an escape route. He went with two other Dutch boys and a South African soldier. No message of their safe arrival came over the radio that evening or the next one. It was not until June, more than a month after the end of the war, that their bodies were found in grazing land. They had gone through the German lines and crossed no-man's-land, so they must have known that they had made it. Then they were killed by a V-1 'doodle-bug' explosion. These early rocket weapons were not always reliable and sometimes hit the ground soon after they were launched. The Dutch suffered from many explosions of doodle-bugs that had been intended for the British.

The fact that Coen did not return meant that we had to find another escape route. It turned out that there was a possible one more to the west, but this called for a half-way house as otherwise the trip would be too long to make in one day. An ideal place was found in Maarn with the Idenburg family.

The Idenburgs were a middle-aged couple. Mrs Idenburg was a placid, kindly person and very hospitable. When they were young her children had always been allowed to bring as many friends home from school as they liked, to play games in the woods, and she gave them marvellous birthday parties. During the war she cooked a hot meal at midday and whoever happened to be there was fed. Apart from her husband, two sons and two divers, there were often half-a-dozen others as well. Cooking was difficult in the last winter of the war as it had to be done on a stove stoked with wood, but she was resourceful and ingenious. She often used to say, 'We are put in this world to help one another,' and she tried to live by this.

She was also shrewd and far-sighted. Her husband's employer – Mr Idenburg was chauffeur to a family who lived in a large mansion – like many Dutch families before the war, had German au pairs staying with them in 1938–9. All these girls had been told by Hitler to collect as many caps off wine bottles as they could (because in those days the caps contained lead) and to bring them back to Germany when they came on holiday. When an au pair asked Mrs Idenburg to keep the caps for her she would reply, 'I am not going to do that because later on my sons may be killed by the bullets that are made of them.'

Mr Idenburg was more irascible than his wife. He told everyone openly that he hated the Germans. Apart from being a chauffeur he also bought old cars, tinkered with them until they were in good condition again and then sold them. He wanted to start a garage with his sons when they had finished school, but the war prevented him from fulfilling this dream.

When the war started, their son Henny had just begun his national service. In those days few people could drive, as there were relatively very few private cars about. Consequently Henny always got the driving jobs. If he was in a convoy and a vehicle broke down, he was the one who had to put it right before they could all go on. When we were invaded he drove lorries loaded with ammunition to wherever they were needed.

Two days after the Dutch surrender he was sent home, and he joined the police. His brother, Cor, was ordered to go and work in Germany, but one day he was given a pass for a few days' leave and at the end of it he got off the train that was returning him to Germany and became a diver at his parents' house. He joined the Maarn Resistance group and towards the end of the war he and his brother moved into a wooden hut in the grounds of the mansion.

Currently, however, Henny was hiding at his parents' house. He had taken his papers, his sergeant's uniform and his gun with him when he became a diver. These were invaluable to the Resistance because policemen on duty could be out during the curfew. A policeman's permit was valid for one month at a time, after which a new stamp had to be put on it. As the Resistance had a good supply of the various stamps, this did not pose a problem.

The Idenburgs' house was in the grounds of their employer's mansion. They had buried the family car in the forest to prevent the Germans from confiscating it. Because the mansion had been turned into a nursing home they had access to plenty of mattresses, so the Idenburgs could take in a number of escapers at any one time. At night, mattresses were put down in the garage for the escapers to sleep on. During the day these mattresses were kept outside. One day a German came to ask what all those mattresses (which some snooper must have reported) were doing there. The Idenburgs told him that they were from the nursing home and had been put there waiting to be disinfected. As usual, the man was scared of catching something nasty and went away quickly.

Mrs Idenburg often had to cook for twelve men, all with hearty appetites. After dinner she would go and have a rest while the escapers did the washing-up.

On 15 January 1945 Henny fetched six Airbornes from Maarsbergen. He thought it very strange that one of them decided not to go any further because, he said, he had to go back to his previous hostess to fetch something he had left behind. Henny was afraid that the man might be a German infiltrator, but as he had the other escapers to look after he could not follow him to check up on him. To his relief the man returned a few days later on his own, but this time speaking fluent Dutch. He turned out to be the British M.I.9 agent Dick Kragt, who had a Dutch father and an English mother (see Chapter 3). He told Henny he had come along to test their escape line. From then on he and Henny worked very well together. Kragt saw to it that groups of escapers linked up at a certain meeting point and Henny took them from there to his parents' house.

Henny was a remarkably cool customer. On 30 April 1945 – a week before the end of the war – he had gone home in the morning to see if there were any messages for him when the Germans pounced on him outside the house, pushed him to the ground and searched him thoroughly. They found nothing, but they still arrested him. They took him to Woudenberg near by and questioned him until nearly 8 p.m., throwing him to the ground and kicking him every now and then, but he gave nothing away. They said they would take him to Zeist, where they had the means to make him talk. Henny was put on a bicycle with his hands tied to the handle bars and a rope was looped through his belt and then tied to the saddle. With a German on each side, they cycled some 13 km (8 miles). When they reached Zeist curfew had begun, so the streets were deserted. Henny had little time left to think what to do.

Of course, Dutch people can do almost anything with a bike. The Germans could only just ride them, and many couldn't do that until they stole one from us. Henny began to vary his speed slightly. He managed to get slightly behind so that the Germans were not completely abreast of him. Then he braked suddenly and made a U-turn. By the time the Germans had stopped, got off their bikes and drawn their guns, he was some distance away. All the shots went astray. Henny zigzagged through some small streets, rode through the gateway of a house and round to the back door, which he let himself fall against. It was not yet dark and a small boy in the garden saw him.

Henny said, 'Fetch your mother and ask her to bring a knife.'

She came quickly and cut him free.

'Have you a hiding-place?' Henny asked.

'Yes, I have a very good one. You'd better come in straight away.'

'Thanks, but they mustn't find my bike if they come searching here.'

'Don't worry. My son will take it through the garden to the neighbours and they will know what to do with it. You just hide and if nothing happens I'll bring you food later.'

Henny stayed all night. Next morning he heard Germans talking. It turned out that they wanted to be billeted in the house. When they left to fetch their belongings, Henny was let out and cycled back through the woods to Maarn. He stayed there in a hut until he thought it would be safe to go home.

Meanwhile the Germans had indeed searched his parents' house again, thinking he might have returned there. They took some of his belongings but found nothing incriminating – his parents had made sure of that. Mrs Idenburg remained very calm and collected during this ordeal, even though she was naturally very worried about her son's safety.

The mistake the Germans had made, of course, was not to have tied Henny's bicycle to their own. Probably they never anticipated an escape. Almost certainly they wouldn't have been very adept at riding a bicycle that was tied to another one.

We help a VIP

Towards the end of January 1945, facilitating the escape of a senior British officer had to be given the highest priority. Brigadier John Hackett had been severely wounded at the battle of Arnhem, taken prisoner and sent to the hospital in Arnhem for surgery. While he was recovering he had been kidnapped by the Resistance and had been hiding in Ede ever since. Dick Kragt and his superiors tried unsuccessfully to find a safe way to get him out. The solution came not from the professionals but from an amateur. Hans van Renkum, a Resistance member who had been evacuated from his home in the Arnhem area following the battle, was the nephew of the women in whose house the brigadier was staying. Hans found a way to cross the lower Rhine near Ammerstol, access to which was strictly forbidden at that time. On the south side of the river Hans located a friend, who told him to go to Sliedrecht. One of the Dutch intelligence organisations, 'Albrecht', apparently regularly took messages and agents by rowing-boat or canoe from Sliedrecht through the Biesbosch to the liberated south of the country.

The Biesbosch is a freshwater delta region consisting of a maze of waterways, creeks and islands, and it made a natural hiding-place for escapers. Koos Meijer of the 'Albrecht' group had worked out a route through the complicated waterways. When the Allied lines reached the River Maas the Biesbosch became the final area to be crossed to freedom, but by this time the task was made much more difficult by the high concentration of German troops there.

Initially the 'Albrecht' group had had to paddle using old canoes, which were liable to make a slapping sound as they moved through the water. Later on, thanks to an American liaison officer, they were supplied with specially built canoes, 6 metres (6½ yards) long and 80 cm (32 inches) wide, which had rounded undersides. These glided almost soundlessly over the water. They were also fitted with electric engines driven by two 12-volt batteries, so that if it was safe to use them it was not necessary to paddle all the way. They usually travelled in pairs, because at one point the canoes had to be carried over a dyke and this was too heavy a job for one crew. If rowing-boats had to be used, the men put sacking or pieces of rubber round the bow, the oars and the rowlocks to dampen the noise. Ducks were a hazard because they were liable to make a terrible noise if they were awaken from sleep and might alert any Germans to the presence of the boats. A total of 440 crossings were made before the end of the war. The trip would take, on average, four hours. The return journey, against the current and usually loaded with supplies, could take all night.

'Albrecht' had never taken an escaper before but they agreed to take the brigadier. In case they needed an extra turn of speed if they should be challenged with him on board, they would use the motorised canoes. Koos Meijer would take the brigadier and 'Alblas' and 'Grey John' would be in the escorting boat.

The date of 3 February was fixed for the crossing, the brigadier was provided with an identity card in the name of Jan van Dalen, and on 29 January Hans van Renkum and the brigadier cycled the first part of the journey from Ede to the Biesbosch. They arrived safely at the Idenburgs' house, where, to the brigadier's amazement, he found several officers from his brigade as well as the surgeon who had operated on him. It was a happy reunion.

While the brigadier was staying at Maarn, word was received from

Coen, 1920–1945
Gerrit Herman Esveld

Chris Cornelisse

Ank Prevo, photo. 1944

Author dressed as a nurse, photo. 1944

C. Idenburgh, 1891–1972
G.J. Idenburgh-Duiveman, 1891–1953

Jan van Dalen
Brigadier Hackett

Good-bye,
many thanks,
Jack R.A.F

"Thanks Holland"
a grateful Australian
R.A.F

"Thanks for Everything"
Tex. A.A.F

"Cheerio" and
Thanks a lot —
Ross R.A.A.F.

Thanks for Everything
Carroll A.A.F.

Thanks for the fine
pancakes and all your
kindness —
Jack
U.S.A. A.F.

In early peace and many
thanks R.C.A.F.

To some swell gals!
Ray U.S.A.F.

Good pancakes
John Cdn Army

Many thanks for your kindness
to us "Ik spreken the besta
Niederlands"
V. Brock Christie
R.C.A.F.

Thanks a million for
your kindnesses
to us. It was well
appreciated
R.C.A.F.

Signatures from Allied airmen collected by Mrs Loudon

'Albrecht' that they could take two more men as well. This meant that an extra guide would be needed. On 2 February Henny came to see me to ask if I was available for the following day. Since I was familiar with the many German guard posts in the area and knew how to avoid them I agreed to accompany the brigadier and Hans (whom the brigadier called John, anglicising his name). We would have to avoid the main roads as much as possible. Dick Kragt would travel separately with the other two officers. I slept that night at my parents' house in Driebergen so that I could be in Maarn early the next morning. Being home again was a bonus, of course, as I didn't see my family very often.

When I arrived at the Idenburgs' I saw a number of British soldiers and tried to work out which one could be the brigadier. I decided he was not yet present, as everyone in the room was too young to hold such a rank. I thought all senior officers were middle-aged at least. Henny went over the route with me once more in case any message had come through about a new German checkpoint, for example, but everything seemed to be 'normal' and straightforward.

Then Henny said, 'You'd better be off now,' and I saw that Hans and one of the British soldiers were saying goodbye and preparing to leave.

'Which one is the brigadier?' I asked Henny, and when he pointed out a young man I thought at first he was having me on. All these British people seemed so casual, so much at ease with one another. There was none of the heel-clicking while talking to a superior officer that the Germans did. Outside we talked about the items I was going to carry on my bike, which included the brigadier's uniform. I fervently hoped I wouldn't be stopped at a checkpoint while I was carrying that!

Then we were off, with me going ahead, as was usual. Bad luck hit us almost at once. We had done only 8 km (almost 5 miles) when I noticed that the others had stopped. I turned round and rode back to them. Hans was looking very concerned. His cycle had a puncture. It looked rather bad as there was a big tear in the outer tyre, so that even if the inner tube could be repaired he wouldn't be able to use the bike. New tyres were completely unobtainable, so the only solution was to try to find another bicycle. Fortunately the puncture happened in the outskirts of Driebergen, so I knew where the cycle shop was in the High Street. However, it was a Saturday morning and the area was busy with people trying to obtain food for the weekend: the shops had nothing to sell, but people came to try to barter something. I hoped I would not be seen by anyone who knew me.

I led the group safely to the workshop behind the shop. It was risky being there, as a Nazi might come in at any moment and want to know what two young men were doing there who ought to have been working for the Germans. Also, I had a British army uniform on my bike, and helping an Allied soldier carried the death penalty. I was anxious to leave as quickly as possible, so we did not spend time on social conversation, even though Mr Reinink knew who I was. He always helped the Resistance, if he could. I showed him the puncture.

'I have to take my two friends some distance and we must get there before curfew,' I explained. 'Can you do anything?'

He shook his head. 'The puncture is no problem, but any repair to so big a tear in the outer tube will take all day.'

'Do you have another bicycle I can borrow and bring back in a day or two?' I asked.

'There's only my own, and I need that to go looking for food for my family this afternoon,' he said.

'Look,' I said, 'please lend me your bike, and go and see my father. He will lend you his if you explain that I have borrowed yours.'

'All right, I'll do that,' he replied, 'I know it's in a good cause. I'll try to mend this bike ready for tomorrow or Monday.'

'Thank you, thank you,' I said, 'I'm most grateful.'

It was very generous of him. Although I had undertaken to return his bicycle, he knew that I could not guarantee to do so. He did not ask any questions: we just trusted each other.

We hurried off. Having made a detour to the centre of Driebergen, we still had some 72 kms of the 80 (43 miles of the 48) to go, and there was no time to lose.

The previous night the temperature had been minus 1°C, so we had hoped it wouldn't be too cold when we cycled during the day. However, the temperature did not rise above 4°C that day and because of the awful time difference the Germans had imposed on us (see page 75) it would be 4 p.m. before the day reached its warmest point. The wind was a moderate westerly, but even though it was not too strong it still meant that cycling a long way against it in so low a temperature made it feel colder than it was. For the brigadier, who was not used to cycling long distances and who had been very ill not long ago, it meant serious exertion. We stopped near Vreeswijk for lunch and ate some sandwiches. Hans had brought four hard-boiled eggs and we all had one. He offered the last one to the brigadier, who said, 'No, thank you.' I had not seen an egg for months and just could not fathom anyone saying 'No, thank you' like that. Funny people, the British!

We reached Ammerstol in the late afternoon without further problems. Although crossing the lower Rhine was strictly forbidden, Hans van Renkum found a skipper who was prepared to do so. He was paid two pounds of wool, which was very much in demand that winter. While the boatman was busy putting his oars into the rowlocks, three other people arrived on bicycles and begged to be taken across too. They had family reasons for wanting to go. We had no reason to refuse them so the boat became rather crowded. There was no risk of these people trying to talk to the brigadier, as he had been given a 'deaf-button' to wear. In the days before hearing aids, the deaf wore these badges to let people know they could not hear what was being said.

The river was at that time 200 m (219 yards) wide. In midstream we had a marvellous view of Schoonhoven in the distance, its spires reaching up into a clear, cloudless sky and the roofs of the houses covered in snow. It looked so peaceful, just like a Christmas-card scene. At a moment like that it was incredible to think that there was a war on.

It took less than half an hour to get across. There was still a lot of ice on the river bank and there were also some ice floes in the river. It was a bit of a scramble but we managed to get out and carry the bikes over the ice. It was only a short distance now to Groot-Ammers, where another Resistance group would take over. I said goodbye to the brigadier and Hans and I was taken by a local Resistance guide to the house of the local GP, where I stayed overnight. The family gave me some bread and butter and even some cheese, which was very welcome. Earlier in the day Dick Kragt had taken the two other British officers along the same route and they, too, had arrived safely.

While the British had to go on the next lap of their journey, I had to return to Maarn the next day. The local Resistance guide suggested that I should travel with Dick Kragt, as it was a Sunday and we had to make our way through a part of the country where people observed Sunday very strictly. They would not think of working then or of riding a bicycle except in an emergency. A man cycling on his own would draw more attention than a man out with a girl, so travelling together seemed a good idea.

Before we had left Maarn, Henny had looked at my bike and declared that it was not good enough for such a risky assignment. Too much depended on it, and as I had to carry the brigadier's uniform and other luggage on my bike the risk of its breaking down had to be minimised. So I had been given a bike with almost new tyres. It was a joy to ride such a beautiful bike and not to have to worry about getting a puncture. Now, however, I had to leave that bike behind, as I had promised to return Mr Reinink's as soon as I could. We left at 6.30 a.m., soon after curfew ended. Dick Kragt had all sorts of useful connections and he had obtained a boat from the Ministry of Works, which looked after dykes and bridges. We did not have to worry about being stopped by Germans as we were now on official business. The skipper of the boat told us how dangerous unauthorised crossings were. A mile upstream at Schoonhoven the Germans had installed a powerful searchlight to look for boats attempting to cross. They apparently knew people were making the crossing and were watching the river more, so we might easily have been detected the previous day. As he went up and down the river most of the day, this skipper was very well informed.

When we arrived at the south bank I found that I could not ride Mr Reinink's bicycle. He was a good 20 cm (8 inches) taller than I was and the saddle was far too high. Foolishly we hadn't stopped to consider this point!

Dick suggested that we call at a cycle shop in the next town and ask them to lower the saddle for us. We did this, but the owner told us it was against his conscience to work on a Sunday. Dick asked him to lend us a spanner, but he refused, saying that giving someone the tools to work with was almost as bad as working yourself. 'Damned Calvinists!' was Dick's comment under his breath. Had we told the man we were working for the Resistance he would probably have counted that as an emergency and have helped us, but we could not risk it. So I had a painful ride back, pedalling without sitting on the saddle. I had also hoped to have the wind at my back on the return journey, but it had changed direction to a south-westerly and had increased in strength. It rained too – later I found out that it was one of the heaviest rainfalls of the month – 'February fill-dyke' indeed!

Mr Reinink was glad to see his bicycle again, though he was even more pleased when my mother gave him half a bucketful of potatoes as a thank-you. He had three small children, a wife, and two Jewish divers to feed, so he needed all the food he could get.

Back in Maarn, I took over my own old bicycle again, which left the beautiful Maarn cycle to be exchanged for Hans's repaired one. That probably never happened.

This may sound like a lot of cycle-exchanging, but in the

Resistance everyone helped everyone else, If a girl had to go on an important mission, the others tried to find the best means of transport. If a cycle was lost to the Germans or through some accident, it was considered bad luck but there were no recriminations.

On 7 February the regular BBC broadcast to the occupied part of the Netherlands included the message: 'The Grey Goose has gone.' That told us that the brigadier had arrived safely in the liberated south. We all rejoiced. It was moments like this that made us feel really pleased with all our efforts.

Using the new route

We now also knew that the new route through the Biesbosch was a good one, except for the weak link across the river at Ammerstol. There was no guarantee that you would find a boatman willing to risk his life. If a boat was stopped and searched and escapers were found aboard, everyone was trapped. You couldn't run away in the middle of the river, and helping an escaper carried the death penalty. So Henny and Dick slightly varied the route.

They would cycle to Vreeswijk along little-used roads, skirting the villages and towns they had to pass. In Vreeswijk there were locks in the river which you could walk across when they were closed. Every morning as soon as curfew ended, many men who were forced to work for the Germans went across to their work. As it was still dark it was not too difficult for the escapers to mingle with them as long as they also wore working clothes.

When the occupation started, the Germans decreed that Dutch clocks were to register Middle-European Summer Time, the same as the Germans had, which meant that the clocks had to be put forward by two hours and forty minutes. In winter it was dark until 10 a.m. and very dark at 7 a.m. when work started.

From Vreeswijk the escapers could cycle on the south bank, under the guidance of the Vreeswijk Resistance group, to Groot-Ammers and from there they could take the same route through the Biesbosch. Henny's group took men to Vreeswijk, usually in parties of five. As the area there was not as thinly populated as Langbroek, it would have drawn too much attention if they had used the same method of travelling with three bicycles as Piet de Springer had done. So five escapers needed five guides, as then the guides took an extra bicycle each on the return journey. Henny, who wore his policeman's uniform, cycled in front. The others followed at some distance, so that they could turn back if Henny signalled to them that it was not safe to go on. The men had to stay in Vreeswijk overnight as it was too dangerous to cross the river in broad daylight.

Whenever a group arrived at a safe house, wherever it was, all the tension quickly drained away. Journeys were very stressful for us all: We never knew what danger lurked round the next bend. Once in our safe houses, though, we didn't have to worry for a whole evening and night. It was like a party starting suddenly, with lots of laughter and the men cracking jokes all the time. One joke about the German propaganda minister was, I remember: 'Do you know Goebbels's epitaph?' Answer: 'Here lies Goebbels. As always.'

Occasionally the boys had a small quantity of alcohol with them and that was the right time to drink it. Everyone forgot their troubles until the next day. It was all right to make a little noise if the house was detached and had a big garden – no one outside was likely to hear it. We all knew the dangers, so everyone was very self-disciplined and things never got out of hand. For those in the Resistance who had had responsibility for the group all day though, this was a precious time to unwind.

Sometimes things did not go all that smoothly. One day five men were delivered to the safe house and collected the next morning. In the meantime four of the Dutch guides went on their way. Henny, however, was ill and running a temperature, so he stayed at the safe house. No sooner had he returned to bed than a member of the local Resistance group came back.

'There's been a sudden checkpoint at the lock,' he said. 'Everyone had to show their identity cards. When they saw what was happening, the five escapers ran off and now we don't know where they are. Look,' he said to Henny, 'you are the only one who has seen them in daylight. You know what they look like. I'm sorry, but can you possibly come and help us to find them?'

It was still dark outside and it would have been hopeless for the others to look for them.

Henny groaned, but he dragged himself out of bed again and went out to search for the missing men. Naturally he did not see any of them for they were all hiding somewhere. So he cycled all round the town and its outskirts whistling *Sarie Marais*, as he thought it was a tune the Americans and British would know.

'I felt like the Pied Piper,' he joked afterwards, but it did the trick. One by one, four men came out of their hiding-places and Henny took them back to the safe house. They were able to make the crossing the next day. What happened to the fifth man no one ever found out. A total of forty escapers went along this new route.

Kirschen (Captain King) left on 22 March 1945 to return to England. At the beginning of April the Allies told the Resistance not to lead any more escapers along this route. The war was so nearly over that taking such risks was no longer justified. We, however, still had to hide these men and feed them!

Awkward customers and tricky situations

The Idenburg family received their escapers not only from Dick Kragt but also from a hospital. After the battle of Arnhem a number of British soldiers were taken to a hospital in Utrecht. When they recovered they were sent to a POW camp in Germany. A contact-man in the hospital's administration told the Resistance whenever a soldier was about to be discharged. Subsequently members of the Resistance would spirit him away and take him to a safe house to await his journey in another direction. The Germans must have been too harassed by their own problems to investigate why and how this loss of their prisoners was taking place so regularly.

The journey from Utrecht to the Idenburgs' house in Maarn generally required three guides. One cycled in front. Should this guide (who usually had good papers) be stopped, the others had time to disappear. A second guide stayed with the group, and the third brought up the rear, to make sure no one was left behind. Couriers regularly used that route, so cycles could be returned by other Resistance members when necessary.

If there were not enough guides available, however, complications could arise. For example, one day there were four British ex-patients and one American, plus one Dutchman who had fought with the Maquis in France. Nobody noticed until the group was almost in Maarn that the Dutchman must have missed a turning and was not there. Jantje Laporte, the courier, started looking for him while the others found somewhere secluded to wait. She cycled back through the woods, hoping he would be hiding there, which was correct as it turned out. She went along whistling a Maquis war song she knew, and lo and behold he appeared from some bushes. What a relief that was! Eventually the whole party did make it to Maarn.

Helping escapers was not always easy. As in every group of people, whatever their nationality, some are nicer than others. Sometimes escapers were stubborn and did not want to listen to members of the Resistance, thinking that they knew better than we did. Some of them did not have a clue about what life was like in an occupied country. Members of the Air Forces were well briefed beforehand: they had an escape kit with maps of all the occupied countries. Unlike Britain, where signposts and names of towns and villages had been taken down or painted out to hinder possible parachutists or spies, the Germans had signs up everywhere to help their own men find their way around. So if an Allied airman saw a signpost he could establish where he was. Airmen also had a phrase book with simple sentences such as, 'I am a pilot. Can you help me?' written phonetically. The soldiers were less well prepared. Some of them did not understand that journeys had to be planned round the phases of the moon. At night, when nobody went out after 8 p.m. or 6 p.m. (curfew times were different in different parts of the country), it was too dangerous to walk about when there was a full moon. Near a river with no houses to prevent a clear view, a German sentry could see for miles around. We couldn't take people across the river if the moon was not right.

One day I was taking a glider pilot from Veenendaal to Amerongen. He was going to be the last one in the party crossing the Rhine that night. It was the last day that the moon was right. His hostess was not a regular member of the Resistance, but she had agreed to put him up for a few hours when we had nowhere else for him. She enjoyed cooking for guests and she also had access to the black market, so she put on a lunch of a kind Dutch people generally had not seen for a long time. She was even making the pilot a special pudding.

When I arrived to collect him the famous pudding was not ready.

'We must go,' I said. 'The timetable is very tight. You'll have to leave the pudding.'

The hostess was distressed. The pilot was stubborn.

'I'm not going without my pudding,' he insisted. 'This lady has gone to so much trouble.'

'Look,' I said, getting exasperated – the Resistance had far more at stake than this precious pudding, after all – 'if you come now you will be home tomorrow and can eat what you like there. Besides, there are the others in your party to think of. You are the last one, and they are all waiting for you. You are putting everyone at risk.'

Nothing I said would shift him. There he sat, waiting for his pudding. I was really annoyed with the hostess for creating this situation in the first place, but I was in no position to argue with her in the circumstances.

'Well,' I said to the pilot acidly, 'in my country it is considered ungentlemanly to keep a girl waiting.'

He remained unmoved. His pudding arrived. He ate it.

I was so angry that I didn't speak to him again until eventually we reached the meeting place in the wood near Amerongen and found that the others had not waited for us.

'There, what did I tell you? Look what a fix you've put us in,' I said angrily. 'You'll have to wait here now while I go and try to get help. Goodness knows what I'm going to do with you.'

I cycled into Amerongen to a local contact I knew and he came with me and took the pilot off my hands. He had to stay there for three weeks until the moon was right again, and he had to be fed. He had had his pudding and that seemed more important to him than the fact that people were risking their lives to help him. I did not bother to say goodbye to him. This was the only really negative experience I had with an escaper, fortunately.

Sometimes quick improvisation was necessary. One day three British escapers were in Jan Lagemaat's barn waiting for me to collect them. Jan distributed food for the Ministry of Food Supply and was still allowed a horse and cart. Without warning, two Germans walked into the shed to commandeer the transport. Jan refused to let them have it and said he needed it for his work. When the Germans would not believe him Jan suggested they should go together to the local Wehrmacht commander to check if they were authorised to take the animal and his cart.

While this discussion was going on, the British pilots, who had not had time to hide, pretended to be doing work in the shed. They picked things up and carried them across the barn to put them down on the other side, and they started to fiddle with agricultural implements that were lying around. When the Germans wanted to know who they were, Jan said they were his employees, also working for the Ministry. The pilots must have looked so convincing, quietly going about their work, that the Germans left and did not even ask to see their permits. Had that happened, they and Jan would all have been arrested. Luckily, too, I didn't arrive on my bicycle while they were there.

In the spring of 1945 there were so many escapers in Leersum that the local courier, Annie, had run out of places to put them. A friend of hers, Mrs Loudon, had a chicken shed in her garden.

'You are welcome to use it,' she said, 'but I really can't spare any food. We haven't enough for ourselves.'

'That's all right,' Annie replied gratefully. 'I'm sure I'll be able to arrange something, if they can stay there.'

So Annie installed some Americans and Canadians and begged food for them from other people. There was a small stove in the shed, so the escapers burned wood in it and did their own cooking.

One day the family was looking out of the window into their garden.

'Look!' said one of them in a horrified tone. 'They are throwing food out of the shed window!'

Sure enough, a saucepan containing bacon was being tipped out into the garden. Apparently they had cooked too much and were throwing out the leftovers.

Mrs Loudon was absolutely appalled. 'I can't remember when my family last had any bacon and here are these boys just throwing it away. Besides,' she went on indignantly, 'other people are going without food and risking their lives for these thoughtless young men. It is incredible!'

I don't think they made the same mistake again. To make amends and to keep fit, they chopped wood and took it in turns to work in the garden. Neighbours were told they were from a deaf-mute institution that had been evacuated out of the war zone.

They couldn't understand that they had to wait until the moon was in the right phase before they could be moved on. Whenever they saw Annie or other girls from the Resistance they hummed *Sarie Marais*, to which they had made up their own words. They refused to tell us what these were until the last moment before they left. The song went like this:

> In days long ago
> Before the Gestapo
> Before men had ever left the ground
> The Spanish Inquisition
> Was the one thing to avoid
> Today it is the Dutch Underground.

I'm not sure that we appreciated those sentiments at the time!

5

Autumn 1944

The autumn started badly for the Resistance in Leersum. At the end of September the RVV courier Jeanne disappeared. Jeanne was a history student at Utrecht University. When in 1943 the Germans decreed that all students had to sign a declaration of loyalty to the Germans, she refused – as did most students. This meant that she was not allowed to attend any more lectures. In those days there were not many women students and the Germans left them alone, so she went back home to Leersum and joined the RVV group.

One evening she left on an errand for the RVV and never returned. The last person who saw her was a boy who had been out after curfew started. He was hurrying home and passed Jeanne, who was standing with her bicycle, talking to a German soldier.

When she did not come home her family went to the police. They arrived with a dog to search the forest near the spot where the boy had seen her. As dogs were also on strict rations they were not allowed to exert themselves unnecessarily. They could not run alongside a cycling policeman but had to be carried in a small cart attached to the policeman's bicycle. The search was to no avail.

Some time later, a German tried to sell a lady's watch and bicycle to a farmer. The farmer was convinced they had belonged to Jeanne. Her sisters went to the local Wehrmacht commander and the soldier was arrested. However, he denied ever having seen her, or having her belongings. The commander decided not to court-martial the man. It was not until November 1946 that her body was found, buried near the place where she was last seen. She had been shot.

Then, in October, there was another disaster in Leersum. One morning, soon after work had begun, several German cars arrived at the council offices and all personnel, including the door-keeper, were arrested. A baker who lived opposite and happened to be passing was also arrested. Nobody knew why. After the war, when incidents like this were being looked into, it turned out that the Germans had been told by one of their spies that arms and ammunition were being kept at the council offices and that the Resistance held meetings there with Allied officers. None of this was true.

The five men arrested were sent to a concentration camp in Germany. None of them would return. Two members of the evacuation committee were arrested at their homes and sent to the transit camp at Amersfoort. They had a terrible time there but they did survive. These arrests were made under the orders of the same SS officer who was responsible for the murder of Mr Noordam at Valkenheide. He had been sent with his troops to the Arnhem area when the airborne landings started. Now that the battle was over, he had returned to plague the citizens of Leersum.

By contrast, at the end of 1944 the Doorn BS group had a stroke of luck. They happened to be carrying out reconnaissance on the edge of the forest where they kept a cache of arms. To their amazement, they saw some German soldiers herding cows along the road. Dusk was falling, so the Dutch group was able to approach the road without being seen. They noticed that one of the cows was lagging behind the rest of the herd, and they were able to isolate her and drive her into the forest, where they killed her. Later the meat was divided between the elderly, the sick, and people with many divers in their homes. No mention of a missing cow was ever made by the authorities. The Germans had either not counted them or must have thought they had made a mistake in their tally. It was a rare moment of satisfaction.

Kors Pater was a forester employed by the Dutch Forestry Commission. He lived with his wife and six of his children in the Leersumse Veld, an area of forest, heath and sand-dunes, with lakes where wild ducks came in the breeding season. The Veld covered 450 hectares (just over 1,100 acres) and Pater's house was isolated right in the middle of it. The Paters were in their late sixties and did what they could for the Resistance. We affectionately called them 'Grandad' and 'Granny'.

The Germans had built a wooden warship in the Veld which they used to teach precision bombing to the Luftwaffe. On days when they were practising, they hoisted a basket on a pole on the road leading to the Veld and no one was allowed to go there. These exercises were not without risk to the local population outside the Veld – on one occasion a German plane crashed, narrowly missing some houses.

One day Germans arrived at Pater's house because they suspected that cars were hidden in one of the nearby barns. The barn belonged to the Forestry Commission. The Germans lined the children and a visitor who happened to be there up against a wall and made Mrs Pater go through the house with them while they searched it. While this was happening, Pater arrived with some rabbits he had found in a poacher's trap. He was totally unafraid of the Germans, and when they started shouting – which was a practice they often adopted – he just said, 'Take it easy. Let me get rid of these animals first.' He put the rabbits down and asked them quietly what they wanted. They wanted the key to the barn.

'I don't have it,' Pater said. 'It is kept in the Forestry Commission's office in Utrecht."

'If you don't give us the key, we shall blow up your house with everyone and everything in it,' the Germans threatened him.

'Well, you'll just have to do it, then,' Pater replied. 'I don't have the key.'

The Germans threatened him twice more. Then they realised that no one would let his wife and children, a visitor, and his house be blown up just for the sake of a key. So they gave up and left, not knowing that Pater had the key in his pocket all the time.

To avoid losing face, the Germans arrested the visitor and took him away with them. Luckily his papers were in order and he was released after ten days.

Hiding places

Two sons of the Paters belonged to the Maarsbergen BS group. They hid the group's weapons. It was easy to dig a pit in one of the many sandy hollows of the Veld. Their pit measured 3 × 4 metres (about 12 square yards) and was supported by poles. They covered it with metal plates and put back on top the soil they had excavated. The entrance was camouflaged by a small spruce tree which had to be replaced regularly as it had been uprooted. Chris Blom had been invited to search for this hiding-place. To make it easier for him, they gave him an area of 10 × 15 metres (150 square yards) to search. He could not find it. So the local group felt fairly confident that, even if the Germans ever searched the area, they were unlikely to find this hiding-place.

The Maarn BS group decided to go one better. They dismantled a small site-hut, dug a large pit, and rebuilt the hut inside the pit. They made a hole in the roof and put a ladder down. The roof had to be camouflaged and all the sand that had been dug up had to be removed without a trace. It was quite a job, but it created a very safe hiding-place. Pilots stayed there while waiting for the right phase of the moon before they moved on, and arms were hidden there.

One of the Maarn group worked in the local council offices. As he was of an age to be sent to Germany to do forced labour, he became a diver. He took the precaution of taking his set of office keys with him, which enabled his group to raid the council offices for blank identity cards and take the town clerk's register, thereby preventing the Germans from being able to identify which men were in the age group to be sent to work in Germany. (This was those born between 1899 and 1926; and, towards the end of the war, those born between 1894 and 1926.) The register was hidden in the Maarn group's hut, which was so dry that the book was returned after the war in excellent condition.

In Resistance jargon we called these pits 'wells'. The Veenendaal group to which I belonged at the time had a particularly large one. It took weeks to build and had three rooms. There was a kind of large entrance hall where a car and two motorcycles were kept. A large corridor led out of this area, with a dozen bunks up the walls, and at the end of the corridor there was a practice firing range 15 metres (about 45 feet) long.

After the battle of Arnhem a Scottish paratrooper called James stayed there for two weeks, waiting for his turn to go home. He taught the group how to handle Sten guns and how to throw hand-grenades. The Allies had dropped Sten guns by parachute, but we did not know how to use them – they were a new weapon to us. And British hand-grenades were different from the German ones. They were probably easy enough to use if you were used to an English cricket ball, but we had never played cricket! James also taught us how to go through the forest without being seen or leaving traces behind. He certainly made himself very useful while he was with us.

If things looked dangerous or there was the rumour of an impending German raid on the area, the group would sleep in their well. They would put out snares for rabbits, which they would cook over a camp-fire. Myxomatosis was unknown then. A nearby farmer would help with other food.

I nearly drown

One night at the end of November 1944 I had to take some urgent messages to my group. George the leader, would be waiting for me near the edge of the forest, just before the curfew started. It was raining hard and it was dark, with just a crescent moon. I was very tired as I had been cycling all day and had not had much to eat. I was cycling along a narrow track next to a canal, when the moon disappeared behind the clouds. I did not see a slight bend in the track. Suddenly there I was in the water! I had ridden straight into the canal!

The shock of the cold water certainly set my adrenalin going. I was furious with myself for letting this happen, and at the same time I was very frightened. There was no one about to help me. If I was going to get out of this mess, I would have to do it myself. It wasn't just a matter of letting go of the cycle and finding a way to climb out. Because of the rain I was wearing a cycling cape – it was a beautiful thick Loden one, generously lent to me by a friend as I had no raincoat of my own – and I had stretched it over the handlebars, with the handles through the slits, to keep my legs drier. Now, in the water, the cape seriously hampered my movements and kept me attached to the bike. I went under the water, struggled to regain the surface, where I snatched a deep breath before I was dragged under again.

I was sure I was drowning. I thought of my parents and of George who would be waiting for me. What would he do when I didn't arrive? Would the group find my body next day or would it be the Germans? Did I have anything incriminating on me? All these thoughts raced through my mind. But the instinct to survive is strong. With a tremendous effort born of desperation, I pushed my legs into the angle made by the frame of the cycle and got enough purchase to tear off the cape. Thank goodness! At least now I could swim, though I had no idea how I was going to climb out. The water was very cold, and I was tiring. But I couldn't give up now. Too many people depended on me. That thought kept me going. I prayed for help, but it was curfew time and no one was likely to come along this lonely canal.

Then the clouds cleared for a moment and in the faint moonlight I identified the bank. It wasn't far away, as it happened. As I kicked out to swim to the bank I felt the bicycle, which must have become stuck on a tree stump or some other underwater obstruction. I had lost all sense of direction while I had been trying to keep my head above water and had probably gone round in circles. I took hold of the cycle, which was too precious to lose, and dragged it with me to the bank. Clutching at tufts of grass and anything else that came to hand, I clambered out, initially holding the bike with my feet, until I was high enough up to have one hand free to pull the machine up after me. I had survived! I lay there by the bank, panting and gasping, soaking wet, of course, but thankful just to be alive.

By the time I felt able to move on, it was raining again. I was too shaken to ride my bike in the dark now, so I pushed it along for another 2 km (about a mile and a half) to the meeting point. To my consternation, there was no sign of George. Now I began to worry that something had gone seriously wrong. I was going to catch my death of cold if I couldn't get inside somewhere soon and dry off. Were the Germans in our part of the forest? Had they caught George? Were they about to come this way and catch me? I doubt if I had ever before felt so utterly wretched. I lost all sense of time and place, but I must have waited for about an hour, trying to shelter from the rain under a tree. Then I heard rustling and the snapping of twigs underfoot. I braced myself. What a relief! I recognised George. He had been delayed – but not by Germans, thank goodness.

I explained briefly what had happened. It was a relief to be able to tell someone, to talk myself out of the state of shock. He took my cycle with one hand and my arm with the other, and he steered me safely to our well. I must have looked a bedraggled, pitiful creature. Luckily someone had a towel and I took a blanket to wrap myself in and went into the empty firing range to take off my wet clothes and dry myself. There was no means of making a hot drink but once I had crawled into one of the bunks the men kept offering me more and more blankets. The last thing I remember before I fell asleep was the terrible smell of my still damp hair.

The next morning it had stopped raining, so a camp-fire was lit to dry my clothes. I was also able to deliver the messages which had been the purpose of my journey in the first place. I usually tried to commit messages to memory, to avoid having incriminating papers on me if the Germans should stop me, so no messages had been lost in the canal.

The beautiful cape, of course, had gone. I felt very bad about that, as there was no possibility of replacing it; but my friend did not reproach me, when she heard how I had nearly drowned. The bicycle could be repaired, which was a blessing. The main point was that I was still in one piece, to carry on my work.

That day I was given some shooting practice in the beautiful range we had in the well. I was handed a Sten gun and practised using it. This turned out to be a waste of time, as I was never called upon to use one, but at the time we had heard that the Maquis in France were fighting alongside the liberation army, and that they had helped the Allies with the liberation of Paris. We thought we might have to do the same in our country, but when it came to it the liberating army stopped just a few miles from us and we were set free without more fighting. I don't know how I would have made out as an infantry woman but I would have done my best if I had had to do it.

Our well remained in use for several months until the local Wehrmacht commander decided he wanted to shoot some of the rabbits, hares and deer to be found in that forest. He brought several dogs with him. As German dogs were not on short rations they could run freely all over the place and it became too dangerous for us to stay there. We had to move the car and the motorcycles, of course. The men put all the group's weapons and ammunition in the car. Then the driver and the man who would stand on the running-board of the car to watch the sky for Allied aircraft – which is what the Germans always did – dressed up in German uniforms, as did the two motor-cyclists who would act as an escort, and they all drove off to a safer place. The move went brilliantly. Of course, our group was taking an enormous risk, wearing enemy uniforms and carrying all our arms and ammunition in one car, but, luckily for us Germans did not think to check the bona fides of other Germans – and the Resistance needed a little luck from time to time.

The Armenians

The wells were sometimes used to hide escapers if they were 'difficult' cases. For example, there were some Armenians in our area. They had been taken prisoner on the Russian front and had almost starved. After thousands of them had died, the survivors were given a choice of working for the Germans or of joining the German army. They refused to fight, so they were sent to work in Poland. They worked at the docks, loading and unloading cargoes. That did not last long, however, because the war was going badly for the Germans. The Armenians were forced to put on German uniforms and carry weapons and to go and help in the occupied countries, thereby freeing Germans to go to the front and fight. Some 2,000 of them came to my country. They were very anti-German, and in the autumn of 1944 they began to desert from the German army.

Some of them were very useful to the Resistance because they gave us weapons. Some, however, gave us big headaches. Hein van Remmerden, the leader of the Doorn BS group, and Jantje Laporte, his courier, brought three Armenians to us from Utrecht to Maarn. Two of them spoke German but the third spoke only Russian. They said the German-speakers were officers and the other one their driver.

Because they looked physically so unlike the Dutch, being dark-haired and swarthy, we could not safely lodge them with a family. If questioned by a neighbour, the family would not have been able to pretend these men were their relatives. Chris Blom knew a small summer cottage that was empty and we took them there. Henny Idenburg, who was leading the Maarn BS group, provided the food.

The Armenians were told to stay inside, out of sight. They took no notice of what we said. The next thing we knew, they had gone outside with one of their rifles and had started shooting rabbits. They were seen by some local people, who commented on it. So we had to move them to the Leersum well. Grandad Pater supplied them with water and the Leersum BS group gave them food. They did not seem to understand anything about the Resistance and what we were doing. They thought we would go around all day shooting Germans, which is what they apparently wanted to do.

Then, on 3 December, a terrible tragedy occurred. A sixteen-year-old schoolboy, Arie Malinosky Blom (no relation to Chris Blom), went out early to look for deer tracks. He was wearing a camouflage jacket from the Marine Steamship Company. He told his mother he would be back for breakfast in an hour, but he never returned. There was a large-scale search for him. Pupils from the local school combed the Leersumse Veld systematically, and Grandad Pater searched with his dog, which had been trained as a police dog. Arie was found four days later, shot through the back of his head.

The local Wehrmacht commander was informed and the murderer was identified. A few days earlier a British plane had been shot down in the area and probably because of the boy's jacket the German had stupidly thought that Arie was the pilot. Had this been so, he could have challenged him and taken him prisoner – the German was armed and the boy was not. Shooting someone from behind was cowardly enough, but to have hidden the body as well, prolonging the agony for the parents, was doubly reprehensible. The Wehrmacht commander suggested that the family could prosecute the soldier, but the Malinosky Bloms said that would not bring their child back and they did not pursue the matter.

As Arie had been found only yards from the Leersum well, the Armenians refused to stay there any longer. George, who was leading our Veenendaal BS group, found an address for them in Veenendaal and asked me to collect them. When I saw them I was appalled. They looked so foreign. One of them had a large black beard, but even with this shaved off it was obvious he was not a Dutchman. I refused to take them unless we had an escort, because I really could not risk riding along with three men who spoke no Dutch and who would stand out a mile as foreigners. I could think of no plausible story to explain them away if we were stopped by a German patrol.

This time the Leersum BS decided that they would have to provide an armed escort. If challenged, we would have to shoot it out. With three men as escort, and myself, we would have four guns – the men had 9 mm Colts and I had a Belgian FN 6.35 pistol (FN stands for Fabrique Nationale) – so we might get away with it. I did not normally carry a weapon, because you could not talk your way out of trouble if the Germans found you in possession of a gun. It was better to try to bluff it out. Nevertheless, if circumstances warranted it I would carry a gun.

The Germans usually went around in twos or threes, though sometimes there were more. I was not happy about this job, but I thought we would have a fair chance if it came to a shoot-out.

We set off. The trip was no joke, for we discovered that the Armenians could barely ride a bicycle. One after another they fell off and at one stage they were all three on the ground at the same time. We proceeded in this fitful fashion for some time, stopping and starting, with the rest of us looking round nervously in case any Germans came along. Not until we were nearly in Veenendaal did the Armenians begin to get the hang of it.

At the outskirts of Veenendaal the escort had to leave us. The military front was now so close that Veenendaal had been declared a restricted zone and only people with a special permit were allowed in the town. I had my permit as a nurse, so I could go where I wanted to. The Armenians would have to take a chance, as we did not have to go far. I told them to follow me and not to talk to each other. To my great relief, we got to the safe house without being challenged. One of the family there was pretending to have diphtheria – this was the time of the diphtheria epidemic in the Netherlands – and they had put a large notice in the window, in both Dutch and German, warning people to keep away. There was no risk of any Germans knocking on their door.

Our troubles were not over, however. One of the Armenians was very pleasant. He turned out to be a vet and was most helpful when a dog belonging to one of the BS group was ill. The other two were very difficult. They played a game using dice all day, and they quarrelled about it. We thought they were probably accusing each other of cheating. They made so much noise that the neighbours heard them and started asking questions. As the Armenians refused to keep quiet, they had to go. This time George walked with them to an isolated farm, but they were still troublesome on the way. One of them behaved as though he was in charge of the others and ordered them about, making them walk behind him and George. But George turned round and started walking between the other two. The leader of the Armenian group could not understand that Resistance people did not order each other about. He kept saying that he was more important than the others as his father was a general and a personal friend of Stalin. Apart from the fact that we were not interested in such claims, there was no way we could check his story.

The Armenians stayed at the farm until the liberation. Even then there were problems. Russians were not supposed to have let themselves be taken prisoner, so they were afraid of being shot when they returned home. They asked for a certificate stating that they had worked for the Dutch Resistance. They had in fact been a terrible nuisance to us, but since they had at least given us their rifles it was true, up to a point, that they had helped us. Thinking that it might save their lives, George wrote a statement for them and I typed out three copies on our ancient typewriter, heading the notepaper 'Interior Forces of the Netherlands, District Utrecht South-East'. The signed certificates looked really quite impressive. The 'general's son' was not satisfied, however, and insisted that his certificate should be longer and better than those for the other two because he was a lieutenant. I said to him, 'Now, look here, you are all communists and you know that means you are all equal and have to share everything.' Well, he couldn't argue with that.

The Armenians went off to be repatriated, and I never expected to hear of them again. Many years later a former member of the Resistance went to the USSR and tried to find out what had happened to them. He met several escaped prisoners who had been in the Utrecht area, and we thought our documents might have saved their lives.

In 1994, in fact, to my immense surprise I learnt from a Dutch journalist, who was researching for a book on Armenia, that 'our' Armenians had made it back home and were not executed. They were court-martialled in 1947 and the lieutenant was sentenced to ten years' imprisonment, which he served in Siberia – so much for his father's reputed friendship with Stalin. The others probably received similar sentences. In 1957 the lieutenant returned home and became a lecturer in a teachers' training college. He still has the certificate I typed out for him and the journalist sent me a photocopy of it. The Armenian had written to his local newspaper about his Dutch adventures and a photograph of him taken at the liberation celebrations before he left us had been reproduced in the paper. I have been told, too, that the Russian NKVD (secret police) apparently didn't believe our certificates and disregarded them, which seems a pity.

Two more Armenians caused even bigger problems to Henny Idenburg at the beginning of December 1944. Henny took them to a local farmer who had a hiding-place in a barn. Although they were told to stay inside, they apparently slipped out late in the evenings to sample the nightlife of Utrecht. Nobody knew about this. The Dutch slept at night and would not go out during the curfew except on urgent Resistance business. The Armenians apparently put on their German uniforms, walked to the road and waited until they heard a motor cycle coming. One of them stopped the motor cyclist, who naturally thought one of his comrades wanted a lift. As soon as he stopped, the other Armenian came up and together they killed the German and took his money and the motor bike. When they returned from Utrecht they put the motor cycle next to the dead man, making it look as though he had swerved of the road and been killed in a road accident.

This was, of course, an extremely dangerous situation. If the body had been found before the motor bike was returned, or if the Germans had conducted a careful post-mortem, they would have known it was not an accident. Also, if it happened too often in roughly the same area, they would eventually have become suspicious about what was going on. The Germans would have blamed the Resistance and taken reprisals locally. Henny found out what was happening only because one of the Armenians asked him to fetch a doctor after the man had visited a brothel. The doctor diagnosed a venereal disease but could not treat it with the few drugs at his disposal. He advised the man to go to a military hospital. Henny also thought that was the best solution. He said he would take the Armenians, in their German uniforms to a main road where they could stop a German car and say they had got lost when their unit moved to Utrecht. Once in Utrecht, they could go to the German military hospital. They agreed but said they would need their rifles back. That was awkward because these had already been given to another group. In the end the rifles were found, the Armenians went to Utrecht and everyone breathed a sigh of relief.

6
The Resistance under Pressure

Living conditions worsen

On Christmas Eve 1944 I had to cycle to The Hague on Resistance business. It was a distance of about 130 kms (78 miles) from Veenendaal, which meant making the return journey on Christmas Day, instead of being at home with my family in Driebergen as I had hoped. It was the worst Christmas I had ever known.

All the way from The Hague to Utrecht I saw women and children with barrows, prams, little carts, anything that could be wheeled. They were walking through the snow, trying to reach a farm where they might be able to buy or barter for food. These trips were called 'Hongertochten' – hunger trips.

The distance between The Hague and Utrecht was 70 kms (45 miles). The building of the motorway had been started but not completed so you could walk or cycle on parts of it, but this was risky because there was a German checkpoint half-way along it and you might very well have everything you were carrying taken from you. It was safer to keep to the minor roads.

The people looked so cold, and they were starving. I had not even enough food with me for myself and I felt so utterly helpless in the face of all this suffering. The family with whom I had stayed overnight in The Hague knew a market gardener who grew grapes – for the Germans, of course. In the evening they had managed to obtain six bunches (riches indeed!) for me to take home. Three bunches were for their son, who was a member of my group, and three were for me, which I was going to give to my mother. Whenever I saw a woman on the road who looked ready to drop, I got off my bike and gave her some grapes. The ordinary people like me had not seen grapes for years. I will never forget how their eyes lit up after they tasted this 'nectar'.

Shortly before this, early in December, I had had another windfall. Some weapons had been dropped near Veenendaal by mistake. They were meant for a group on the Veluwe, but the pilot had lost his bearings. Fortunately a member of the local Resistance spotted the drop and called some others to help gather it up. They worked all night and hid it away safely. In the aftermath I had to take some guns to an address and was given a share of the goodies the British had dropped along with the weapons. This turned out to be 50 grammes (2oz) of tea – often they dropped cigarettes and chocolates.

I was ecstatic about my prize! I would have liked to have kept the tea until Christmas, to give it to my mother, but if anything had happened in the interval, such as a sudden move to another district, or even being caught by the Germans, she would never have received it, so I took it to Driebergen straightaway as a surprise. My mother believed in the Commandment: 'Love thy neighbour as thyself'. She meant this literally and always shared whatever she had managed to obtain with others. Even though we were going short ourselves, she would still give to those who had less. She always said, 'Giving has never made anybody the poorer.' So the nice thing about it from my point of view was that she could not share this gift – she could not explain to anyone outside how she had acquired English tea. With great ceremony she made a pot. She had so often said, 'How I long for a cup of real tea.' It tasted wonderful!

My young sister Ank was there, of course, and she could not remember ever having tasted tea. When she was small she had drunk milk and when she was older tea was unobtainable. She was greatly looking forward to having a cup of this famous brew now. It was not until I came to write this book that she told me she had not liked the taste of it at all at the time. Tea is something you have to get used to, after all.

By February, rations were down to only 500 calories a day, which is a mere 20 per cent of what an adult needs. My mother kept the family fed by bartering. When the war was over, my brother, sisters and I had none of our childhood toys left; no teddy bear, no favourite books. Most of the household linen and anything else that could be spared had also gone.

By this time too, washing your hair was almost impossible. There was no shampoo and no hot water. To dry your hair you had first to rub it with a towel that was almost threadbare after five years of war – the good towels were bartered for food – then you had to crouch in front of a wood-burning stove, without taking all the heat from the

93

others in the room. It was better to wait until the spring and let your hair dry naturally in the sun.

Trouble in Langbroek

On 30 December 1944 what might have been just a minor brush with a couple of German soldiers suddenly escalated into a major incident. It turned out to have extensive repercussions, especially in the Langbroek area, where hitherto the Resistance – in particular, the radio operators – had been able to work relatively easily. Our network there began to unravel dangerously.

At 11 o'clock a German sergeant-major and a soldier, who were stationed in Doorn, came to Gerrit de Jong's hairdresser's and tobacconist's shop in Langbroek – where I had stayed earlier – and asked for cigarettes. They probably only wanted to try to buy some black-market supplies. Gerrit said he had no cigarettes and would not have any more until the following week when a new coupon would become valid on the ration card. The Germans didn't believe him and said they would come and find the cigarettes for themselves. They pushed through to the sitting-room in the house behind the shop. There they spotted an opened carton of cigarettes on the mantelpiece which De Jong had saved from his own rations. They thought there would be more hidden away, so they started to search the house.

While Gerrit waited in his sitting-room with the soldier, the sergeant-major went into the kitchen, where he found, hidden in a drawer, some ammunition. He immediately went out to fetch reinforcements.

After a while, the soldier, wondering what was happening, said to the barber's assistant, 'Where's my comrade?'

'He's gone,' the assistant answered.

So the soldier went outside too, to look for the sergeant-major, and immediately the barber's assistant left through the back door, calling to Gerrit to go with him.

De Jong, however, did not want to leave his wife alone with the Germans, so he hesitated. He did not know about the ammunition, because someone else had left it there, and he thought the only problem he had was in having refused to sell the Germans cigarettes. While he was thinking what to do, the sergeant-major came back with an officer and another soldier. It was only then that Gerrit heard about the ammunition.

The only customer in the shop had come for a shave. With half his

94

Kors Pater 1876-1960
Klara Pater-Pater, 1879-1970

Gerrit de Jong and Cora de Jong-De Bree and their shop in Langbroek

face still lathered, he so obviously looked the genuine article that he was allowed to leave.

Soon after this Kees ten Wolde, the local school headmaster, arrived. He had gone that morning to his in-laws in Utrecht, as they had managed to obtain some clothes for the baby his wife was expecting. Because there was no public transport and no postal service, it was usual that if someone was going into town he or she did errands for others in the village at the same time. Cora de Jong, who was pregnant, had asked Kees to deliver a letter to her gynaecologist in Utrecht. She could not possibly have cycled the 20 km (12 miles) to the clinic and back.

When Kees entered De Jong's house through the back door to report on his visit to Utrecht, he was suddenly confronted by a German with a revolver in his hand. He had to put his hands up and go to the sitting-room where he was searched. His papers were checked and he was questioned about why he had come to the house. As he could show the Germans the baby clothes he had with him, his story sounded plausible enough. Fortunately he had nothing on him to connect him with the Resistance, of which he was, of course, a member. He was not, however, allowed to leave. This was disastrous, as otherwise he could have warned everyone not to go near the shop.

When the Germans left the room for a moment, Gerrit told Kees that they had found ammunition in the kitchen and that would mean he would be shot. Both Cora and Kees urged Gerrit not to do anything hasty but to bide his time. They would try to think of a way out.

Early in the afternoon De Jong was told he would be taken to the German headquarters in Doorn. The temperature outside was around freezing point and there was a lot of snow. Kees, who spoke German fluently, asked if De Jong might fetch his coat. Permission was granted and the Germans let him go unaccompanied to his bedroom, where he had said the coat was. Gerrit walked noisily up the stairs and then crept quietly down again. He left through the kitchen. Behind his house was a narrow path that led to the cemetery, and from there he went across the fields to Leersum.

Cora and Kees meanwhile had been keeping up an animated conversation to draw attention away from the time it was taking for Gerrit to fetch his coat. When eventually the Germans thought of investigating, they found the bird had flown. They were furious, of course, and proceeded to search the house very thoroughly. They lifted the carpets and emptied out all the cupboards. Under the floorboards in one room they found a radio and in one of the cupboards two pistols, a police uniform, some blank identity cards and some permits. Now the fat was really in the fire. One of the permits was from the Ministry of Food, exempting Dirk Jan Meyer from working for the Germans. The town clerk was fetched and he was asked if he knew a Dirk Jan Meyer, but of course he didn't.

At 3.30 p.m. Piet de Springer, who had no idea that the Germans were there, arrived at the house. He had just taken two British soldiers across the Rhine. His papers were excellent, but unfortunately his permit was also from the Food Ministry and was in the name of Piet Jan Meyer. This naturally made the Germans very suspicious and they ordered him to stay. They questioned everyone. Cora kept telling them she knew nothing about all this, which was true. She said everything in the room where the incriminating things had been found belonged to a lodger she had taken, in to make ends meet when the ladies' hairdressing salon had had to close because there was no more shampoo or hot water. Her lodger worked for the Food Ministry and he was away because of the New Year weekend.

It turned out later that someone had put the ammunition in the kitchen and the pistols in the cupboard that morning temporarily, intending to fetch them that evening. This was not only a stupid thing to have done but it was also unfair on the De Jongs. If weapons were going to be left at a house, the family should have been told. If Gerrit had known about the arms he would have given the Germans his own cigarettes to avoid antagonising them, or he would have slipped away, taking Cora with him, when his assistant did, leaving his business and hoping they would not wreck everything.

The Germans said that everyone would now have to go with them to Doorn. Piet whispered to Kees that he had some very important signals in the frame of his bicycle under the saddle and that it was essential they did not fall into enemy hands. He had hoped Kees could take his cycle, but now the Germans wanted Kees to go along as well.

Piet then told Kees: 'I don't want them to get me. I know too many names and don't know if I can hold out under torture. I'll see to it that they won't get me alive.'

There was only one opportunity for Piet to escape. Kees asked permission to go and use the lavatory. The German who was at the front door had to accompany him. As soon as the German left his post, Piet ran out to the front of the house and jumped on his bicycle, but because of the snow and ice the road was like glass and the bike slipped, causing Piet to fall. The German who had accompanied Kees heard the front door being opened, and he ran to it and fired. Piet was hit in the back and the bullet went through his chest. He died instantly. If he had left his bike and just run, he might have escaped. His great sense of duty was his undoing. We never knew if the Germans found the messages in the frame of Piet's bicycle or how important they were, but since there were no immediate repercussions in our area, it is likely that they never thought to dismantle the bicycle.

The Germans carried Piet in and put him down behind the counter in the shop. They searched his clothes and his boots but found nothing. They were furious that now they couldn't question him. The soldier who had shot him said he had aimed at Piet's legs but because of the fall the bullet had gone through his back.

At 6 p.m. Cora, Kees and the maid, whose name was Janny, were made to start walking to Doorn. By then it was freezing much harder and it was difficult to walk the 3 km (1.8 miles) to the police station. As Cora was pregnant she obviously needed support, so Kees and Janny were allowed to take her between them. The Germans followed, some 40 metres (44 yards) behind, with their rifles at the ready. As the prisoners walked along they were able to agree what they would say when they were questioned. Cora impressed on Janny that whatever she was asked she should say she had never seen or heard anything. Both would say that Kees was a visitor who had come to tell her about his trip to Utrecht. As this was the truth, that was the easy bit. There was no reason for the Germans to suspect that Kees belonged to the Resistance.

When they reached Doorn, Cora was interrogated first. Whatever she was asked, she alternated between two replies: 'I don't know' and 'I really don't know'. Janny was in another room, where a German was playing with his revolver to intimidate her. She succeeded in convincing the Germans that she only went to the house to work and had never seen or heard anything. She and Cora both insisted that Kees was just a visitor.

Next morning Cora was taken to the prison in Utrecht. Janny and Kees were freed. When Kees was given his papers back, he was told that he was very lucky not to have fallen into the hands of the Gestapo.

Kees walked back to Langbroek. The Germans were still at the De Jongs' house, but Kees was allowed to take his bicycle and the baby clothes. The Germans had intended to set fire to the house, but the town clerk persuaded them not to. He said the house did not belong to De Jong and if they burned it down they would be hurting the owner but not De Jong.

The distress and alarm of the Resistance in Langbroek was considerable. De Jong's assistant knew about his employer's membership of the Resistance but he did not know who the local leader was or where to find other members, so he was not able to alert anyone to what was happening. Since he was a diver himself, he left the area for another safe address.

The Alberts family, who might have been able to warn Piet de Springer not to go to the De Jongs' house if they had been at home and had been aware of what was going on, had moved away to Leersum. The Germans had built a large radio installation on top of Dirk Alberts's grain silo – Dirk was a corn merchant, though most of his corn had been confiscated. Piet de Springer had reported this installation to London and had advised the family to move out, as their house might be bombed. Dirk still came to his office every day – he was over fifty years old and therefore exempt from having to go to Germany to work – and his daughter Dit worked there too, but it was a Saturday and the office was closed.

The half-shaved customer at the shop had raised the alarm by calling at the Swaluwenburgs' farm and telling them that the Germans were searching at the De Jongs. Dit Alberts happened to be visiting the farm and she set out to call at all the places where Piet might be, but she had not been able to find him. It seems that completely by chance Piet had entered the village that day by a different route, so no one could have warned him.

The Resistance did not think it likely that De Jong had been betrayed. Had that been the case, the Germans would not have needed the pretext of buying cigarettes; neither would they have gone there without an officer in charge. The group thought it could probably carry on as usual. After all, Kees ten Wolde had been released the next day.

There were other repercussions, however. With the death of Piet de Springer the wireless operators Wiebe and Gerrit (Schotanus) had lost their controller and could not continue with their work. Wiebe had been on leave for the weekend and did not hear the news until 2 January. He decided not to return to Langbroek but to work elsewhere. Gerrit had also been away that day and he, too, decided to leave. That left Jeanne van Kleef with the transmitter at her farm. She packed it in straw, walked a long way through the fields with it and hid it under a bridge. It was three weeks before Gerrit thought it safe enough to go and collect his equipment. Dick Last slept that night in a chicken coop behind the Jacobshoeve and waited until more was known about what had happened. He then found that he could not make his usual radio connection with London. They were probably afraid that he had also fallen into German hands and that his transmitter was no longer reliable. Dick left for the Veluwe and worked there for Dick Kragt until the end of the war.

This marked the end of Langbroek as a radio station. The Germans would be extra alert now to what went on in that quiet and remote village. They still did not know how a hairdresser and tobacconist had acquired two pistols, a policeman's uniform and a bunch of forged papers, and no doubt they were investigating. It would have been foolhardy for the Resistance to have continued with radio traffic from that area after these unsettling events. Without knowing it, the Germans had dealt a major blow to the local Resistance by shooting Piet de Springer.

Dit Alberts had taken some of her books to Gerrit de Jong's for safekeeping when her family had moved out of their home, expecting it to be bombed. One of these books had her name and address in it, so when the Germans who were searching at the De Jongs' house found this book they wanted to know what the connection was between the De Jongs and Dit Alberts. They went to her father's corn merchant's office to talk to her but fortunately she was not there. The Germans left a message that she was to come and see them. Wisely she decided not to obey. She took a new identity and left the district.

Nobody knew the real identity of Piet de Springer. Even if they had known it they would have been foolhardy to admit it. No one would have dared say that Piet had stayed with them, even though there were several addresses where he had regularly slept. So the only person who could safely go to the council offices and register his death was the local undertaker. Police Sergeant Bouw had taken statements from the neighbours across the road who had seen what had happened, but five days passed before, on 4 January, Piet's death certificate was issued. This described him as 'unknown male, approximately thirty years old'. It was not until the end of June, almost two months after the liberation, that his parents heard about the tragedy. In 1946 Piet's death certificate was amended by a court order and his real name, Jan de Bloois, and other details were added.

Everyone was very concerned about Cora de Jong, who was

expecting her first baby. No one could find out what was happening to her, but it turned out that her gynaecologist also acted as a doctor to the prison in Utrecht. Since Dit was no longer available as a local courier, I was asked to cycle over to Langbroek from Veenendaal, where I was now based, to see Kees ten Wolde. He knew who Cora's gynaecologist was and explained to me how to get there. I was given several ration cards to take with me, in the hope that they would help to obtain extra food for Cora.

I arrived in Utrecht very tired, having cycled for over three hours through the snow, with the roads in an appalling state. My legs really ached and I felt as though I couldn't push those pedals round any more. I hoped to be able to ask the doctor if I could rest there for half an hour before I set off to return to Veenendaal. Oh dear, it soon became obvious that I was not going to be given that chance. The doctor's attitude was very cold. She did not want to listen to any suggestions about providing Cora with extra rations.

'I never accept unofficial ration cards,' she said; 'not for anybody, however great the need.'

Her response was understandable. I could have been an *agent provocateur*, trying to find out if the doctor worked with the Resistance. She could not check my story that I had come on behalf of friends in the Resistance – though I was, of course, putting my life in her hands by telling her this. However much I pleaded with her to take the cards, she would have none of it.

I was desperate, despondent and almost in tears. It was so frustrating. There was my friend Cora, languishing in prison and not having the food she needed for the baby, while I had ration cards I could not give her. Defeated, I turned back to the door, and then in desperation I put the cards down on a nearby table.

'They are not mine,' I said. 'They were given to me for Cora de Jong. You may as well have them.'

As I was going out and closing the door, the doctor said in a kindly voice, 'I'll see if I can do something for your friend.'

We found out later that Cora had in fact received extra food.

As Cora kept on denying she knew anything, she was at last believed and was allowed to go home. But home was home no more. The Germans had stolen everything in the house, even the pram, the cot and the baby clothes. Friends had offered the Germans money for the layette but they refused to sell. The local police had taken away the hairdresser's equipment and put that in a safe place so that the De Jongs could carry on with their business after the war. Cora went into hiding in case the Germans decided to re-arrest her. Her baby was born a few weeks after the end of the war.

Appearances are deceptive

It was lucky that Cora was released, because she was able to tell the Resistance what questions she had been asked. She warned me that my name had come up several times. The Germans apparently had a very good description of me. When one German had asked Cora if she knew a girl called Elsa, who had dark hair, another interrogator had remarked: 'she is dark today, fair-haired tomorrow and a redhead the day after. One never knows what colour hair she has.' I had only once dyed my hair from black to red, so possibly the Germans were testing Cora to see if she would react.

Apparently a few weeks after Cora's arrest a man who had worked with the Veenendaal group had been stopped because he was riding a motor cycle. There was a discrepancy between his identity card and the permit for the motor bike. When he was questioned he did not hold up very well and, no doubt hoping for a lenient sentence, he gave the Germans the names and addresses of several members of the Veenendaal Resistance and also a description of the Veenendaal girl courier called Elsa. Fortunately I had never told him my real name or where I stayed, but he knew I had dyed my dark hair. On an earlier occasion, too, when my name had been mentioned the description was of a girl with dark hair, so that is what the Germans were currently looking for.

George had advised me to change the colour of my hair. This was not easy, as hair dye was no longer available. My friend Ank knew a hairdresser who had some peroxide, but I was so dark it needed rather a large quantity – more than the hairdresser had. Instead of going blonde, I had therefore to settle for red hair. The peroxide caused blisters, but they healed up quickly. To check that I really did look different I went to visit my grandfather. He failed to recognise me so I was confident that my new persona would work.

Knowing that the Germans had my name, 'Elsa', I had to change that too. That wasn't difficult, because there were many evacuees from Arnhem in Veenendaal and many of them had lost their papers during the fighting. They were issued with new identity cards. I had to make an appointment to go to the council offices, to see one of the officials in the town clerk's office who worked with the Resistance. I told him I had lost my papers when a bomb had hit our house. Although he might have enquired why it had taken me so long to come forward with this story, he asked no questions, and issued me with new papers as an evacuee from Arnhem. Of course I gave him a false name – Louise van Dam – address and date of birth, and these then became official, as did my false profession as a midwife. I would be fairly safe at any checkpoint, provided the Germans did not have my description in their hands at the time. You can't take measures against every eventuality.

More arrests

Meanwhile there had been more bad news. On New Year's day the courier Bep Labouchère had called at the Swaluwenburgs' farm to tell them that Jacques and Kees, the two wireless operators who had worked from there for a while, had been arrested. It was sheer bad luck. They had been on their way to their transmitter, which was hidden in a forest, when they met a German patrol who were out looking for an arms cache. A Resistance worker who had been terribly tortured had told the Germans that weapons were hidden in the forest. The Germans were suspicious of these two men walking there and arrested them. While they were driving them to their headquarters, Kees jumped from the car and was shot. Despite his injuries, he was subjected to harsh interrogation. He died a few weeks later in a German military hospital. Jacques was also questioned but gave nothing away.

On 8 March the Germans decided to take reprisals for an attack on General Rauter, who was head of the SS and the German police in the north west. In the Veluwe they shot 117 men. Jacques was one of them, so were Van der Hoop and Jan Thijssen (Lange Jan).

When the Airborne landings at Arnhem had been announced over the radio the previous autumn, Piet de Springer, Jacques and Kees had danced round the table and had told Farmer Swaluwenburg: 'Now we have a fifty per cent chance of making it.' Alas, none of them did.

Girl couriers

That last winter we couriers had a tough job. It was no joke cycling on what were by now old, ramshackle bicycles, which were often fitted with wooden tyres because the original rubber ones had long since worn out. When Dick Kragt saw the sorry state of my tyres, he promised me some new ones. The prospect really cheered me up and I looked forward to this treat eagerly. The tyres were sent with an arms drop from Britain, but when Dick came to see me after the war

I had to tell him they had never reached me. They had been passed down the line all right, but for security reasons the message about who was to have them was only a verbal one. Somewhere along the way my name was dropped from the message, so 'the girl courier' who received the tyres was no doubt made very happy! Not so me!

We really had to exert ourselves, and we often had little food to look forward to at the end of the day. We cycled through rain, snow and freezing cold temperatures, most of us by then without boots or a shower-proof coat. Sometimes our clothes were so wet that they did not dry overnight. For safety's sake we had to avoid main roads, which made each trip much longer than by the more direct way.

Couriers not only took messages and letters but also transmitters, explosives, weapons, or whatever was required. We had to be resourceful and flexible the whole time. One morning my bike got a puncture and I was an hour behind schedule. I was very annoyed and I decided the only way to catch up was to leave out one outlying farm. I would call there on my afternoon round instead.

When I finally arrived at this farm I discovered that the farmer had been arrested that morning, along with all the male evacuees from Arnhem who were staying there. If I hadn't had that puncture to deal with and I had arrived on time, I would very probably have been arrested too, as I was carrying the reports of German troop movements of the previous day and night – the intelligence reports of that area – which I would not have been able to explain away if my baggage had been searched. The farmer died in a concentration camp, as did the evacuees. The farmer knew the risks he was running when he joined the Resistance, but the evacuees had only just arrived and were not involved in anything anti-German. They died not even knowing why.

We had to keep our wits about us. One day I was cycling over the heathland near Maarn, carrying a radio transmitter. You could not hide such a bulky piece of equipment, so there it was, sitting on my luggage rack. Suddenly I was stopped by two Germans, who wanted to see my papers and to know what I was doing there. I showed them my papers, told them I was a nurse and gave them my brightest smile. Then I pointed up at the sky, which as luck would have it was gloomy and overcast, and said, 'Sorry, I'm in a hurry. It's going to pour with rain in a minute and I don't have my mac with me.' I jumped on my bike and rode quickly away. I had distracted them sufficiently and they had not thought of investigating my luggage. They probably assumed it was medical equipment. In fact one of the Germans called after me, 'You'd better go as fast as you can.' I waved my hand in a friendly way, without turning round, and pedalled hard.

The Germans were less likely to suspect girls because, unlike young men, they were not called up to work for the Germans. They would want to know why young men they saw out and about were not at work. Also the Germans generally thought of women as just having a domestic or decorative role in life. They did not realise how many girls had joined the Resistance. Of course, if a woman was arrested because she was in the Resistance the Germans did her no favours at all.

A daring rescue

That winter the Resistance had one major success. In Zeist, a town between Utrecht and Driebergen, a Jewish couple, who had good papers, were trying to live 'normal' lives in an ordinary house. They had two sons, who went to school in Driebergen. The younger boy attended my father's school. My father had enrolled him under a different name and no one was any the wiser. At the beginning of January the family decided to try to obtain some food from a farmer. The mother and her two sons set off, leaving her husband behind. Unfortunately they were stopped and arrested by some Germans who thought they looked Jewish. When they did not return, the father sought help from the Resistance. A friendly contact at the police station told the Resistance that the woman and her boys were there, as were some other Jews. There were ten of them waiting for the Germans to take them away, and this would happen on 23 January.

The Resistance in Zeist decided that it would be possible to free them but it could not be done by local men, who might be recognised. It would be safer if the police could tell the truth afterwards and say they did not know the men involved. The regional commander of the BS asked Henny Idenburg for help. Henny was not known in Zeist and, as a former policeman, he knew how to behave convincingly in a police station. He could also drive, which few people could do at that time. During the war young men had no opportunity to learn.

There was, you may be surprised to learn, a Luftwaffe corporal called Rudi hiding in Zeist and known to the Resistance. He had deserted because he disagreed profoundly with Nazi doctrines. He was now asked to help with this rescue.

The Resistance needed somehow to obtain the use of a German truck to transport their 'prisoners'. There was a large garage at which the mechanics were forced to do work on German vehicles, and someone there 'accidentally' broke a window in a truck. It had to be taken elsewhere to be repaired and the garage owner agreed to turn a blind eye if this truck was 'borrowed' for an hour. So the rescue had to be done expeditiously and the truck returned quickly.

On 23 January, when the Jewish group were due to be taken away, Henny, in his policeman's uniform, and Rudi, wearing a German uniform, went to the police station and said they had come to collect the prisoners. As the Germans were expected, the police assumed that Henny and Rudi were genuine. Henny handed over the necessary papers, which were forged, of course, and Rudi told the police to look sharp and hurry up. Rudi knew exactly how the Germans always shouted at the Jews and abused them, so when they were brought out of their cells he duly roared at them and pushed them none too gently into the waiting truck. Members of the Zeist Resistance had hidden themselves all round the police station to help if anything went wrong, but they were not needed.

It was all done so convincingly that the police said afterwards the German escort had been real brutes. Henny drove to a place near the forest between Driebergen and Zeist. There, members of the Driebergen Resistance were waiting to take the party to a church, where they stayed for several days in the vestry before being dispersed to safe addresses. It was not until they got out of the truck that these poor frightened people knew they had been freed. When the truck had stopped near the forest they had thought they were going to be shot. It was a very traumatic experience for them but unless it had looked like the real thing the escape plan would not have worked. All of them survived the war. The Dutch police had acted in good faith, having been given the proper papers, so they were not blamed for handing over the prisoners.

Some light relief

Occasionally we did have a break from our work, to relax and enjoy some fun. On 31 January I went to a marvellous party in Driebergen. A friend of mine was getting engaged and I knew his fiancée too. The date was the birthday of Queen Wilhelmina's granddaughter Beatrix, the present Queen. Because of the curfew the party lasted from 8 p.m. until 6 a.m. It was held in the house of the girl's parents, which was a safe address. The family were seven, including the fiancée, and there were about a dozen guests.

Every effort had been made to decorate the room. You couldn't buy decorations anywhere but much ingenuity had been used to create a pleasant effect. One of the men had obtained a condom, which he had blown up and hung on a piece of string. The hostess was touched that he had managed to find a balloon, even if it was a small one – she never found out what it really was!

The family had asked a baker to bake an apple pie for the occasion. You had to supply the ingredients yourself, of course, as no baker could provide them – but he did have a hot oven. A farmer had sold them some apples and they had somehow put together the rest. After the pie was baked, however, there was a frightful calamity. It had been put on a very low shelf to cool and a customer – who was known for his clumsiness – walked backwards while he was talking to the baker and trod on it! Well, there was no question of throwing it away; it was far too precious for that. It was not until long after the event that I found out the bit of heel-print on my piece was not a manifestation of cubic art.

It was so long since we had had a party. It went with a swing right from the start. We had a singsong, played some games and at midnight had something to eat. One of the girls had a beautiful soprano voice. She sang some songs, one of them being her boyfriend's favourite. It was about longing for the spring, which we associated with liberation. 'If only you could always hear the singing of spring, deep in your heart and above your head.' A few weeks later her boyfriend was shot during a raid; she never sang that song again. At 6 a.m. I went to my parents' house to sleep for a few hours, and then it was back on the road again.

I had felt so cheerful that night. For once I could forget all the misery of the past months, forget that only a month ago Piet de Springer had been shot. I did not want to think about what might lie ahead. Now was now, and I was jolly well going to enjoy myself.

My mother was even more unlucky with the same baker. Ten days later it was her birthday. She had managed to obtain two eggs – I wondered what she had had to barter for them, they were so precious – which she took with a bread and a margarine coupon to the baker, to make a cake. Of course the cake would turn out smaller than the ingredients allowed, but it was only fair that the baker would take his share for his heating and effort. The cake, however, failed to arrive. My sister Ank went to the shop and was told that there had been a mistake. There was no cake. Someone had used the eggs for something else. The baker returned the coupons but said he could not possibly replace the eggs. My mother was very philosophical – she did not insist – but we were all very disappointed.

Hunger and sickness

Food became a terrible problem that winter. The Germans requisitioned from the farmers whatever food there was. They did not care if the Dutch starved. Many farmers would gladly have shared what they had with the hungry but they had no chance to do so. The Resistance decided it would have to do something about this. They forged the form the Germans used, went to the farmers and asked for the food. The document, an official requisition form with all the necessary stamps and signatures, would state the amount of meat, corn, cheese, potatoes, and so on, that the farmer had to hand over. He would give the Resistance the food and then when the Germans came he could show them a proper receipt and say some other unit had already been there.

At the beginning of February the Resistance in Maarn acquired in that way 2,800 kg (almost 3 tons) of corn. This was split with some other nearby villages. Transport was tricky because of the snow, and most of it was carried on small sledges. Two bakers worked very hard and baked great quantities of loaves. Maarn's share had been 630 kg (almost 800 lbs). There was no more salt, but a member of the Maarn Resistance knew where the railway kept the salt it used to defrost its points. Although the five-month-old railway strike meant there were no trains for the Dutch, the Germans still ran trains, so the salt was still there. The bakers managed to remove most of the dirt from it and to those who were starving the bread tasted marvellous. The vicar, doctor and district nurse were asked by the Resistance to oversee fair distribution of the bread so that only the really hungry received it.

Sometimes a farmer was unwilling to co-operate. In that case the Resistance would send a small group to the farm in the evening, masked and armed, and they would force the farmer to give up the food. This was done only *in extremis*, when people were really desperate for food.

An additional problem was created by the arrival of many evacuees. In September 1944, 500 of them had come to Langbroek from the Arnhem area and in the following January another 750 arrived from the Betuwe, which the Germans had flooded. This almost doubled the normal population. In Driebergen 2,000 evacuees increased the population by 20 per cent. The Arnhem evacuees had arrived while the weather was still good, but the ones from the Betuwe arrived in appalling conditions. Those without bicycles had to walk all the way, a distance of some 40 km (25 miles). Old people travelled on open carts. No one had thick socks or good shoes by this stage of the war, so many people had frost-bite. A temporary hospital was set up in what had been a boarding-school until the children had been sent home. Beds were available and some blankets, but there were no bandages or drugs or other essentials for the running of a hospital. People did the best they could to improvise.

A local doctor was put in charge and he worked in very bad conditions. There was no soap, nothing for cleaning floors or beds. Many people had lice or scabies. There were no ambulances. If someone was so ill that he or she had to be taken to the hospital in Utrecht or Zeist, a stretcher was put on a carrier-tricycle. Two volunteers were kept on stand-by to cycle to town with the patient. All other forms of transport had been stolen by the Germans.

Everyone was very thin and debilitated – half-starved, in fact. Most of them were anaemic and consequently had low resistance to infection. Some had been eating scraps they had found in the dustbins of a German meat factory – the Germans still had meat, and the scraps were made into sausages. Rubbish was not being collected any more, so the scraps were far from fresh, and now these desperate people were suffering from food poisoning. Two patients died because they had eaten hyacinth bulbs. It is safe to eat tulip bulbs but not hyacinths. The newspaper even gave recipes for tulip bulbs. This advice appeared on 22 January 1945, so you can tell how desperately hungry we were long before the war ended.

Storage: keep bulbs dry, preferably in an attic. Turn them every other day. Don't turn them if they are frozen.
Preparation: take the outer skin off, halve the bulb and discard the yellow kernel. Cook them like potatoes. They should be ready in 8–15 minutes.
Stewing: take 2 kg (4 lbs) bulbs, 2kg (4 lbs) potatoes and 4 kg (8 lbs) red cabbage. Cook the bulbs separately from the other ingredients. Stew the potatoes and cabbage together, and then mix everything together.
Soup: cook 2 kg (4 lbs) of bulbs. Add 5–6 litres (10–12 pints) water. Add salt and green vegetables.

In March 1945 I went to see Annie, the Leersum courier. She was staying at Mrs Loudon's. Annie and I made a number of trips together, finding and carrying food to her parents. In the snow we used sledges and if there was no snow we used children's toy carts, called 'vliegende hollander' – which are like go-carts, but you propel them by using your arms not your feet. Annie had just obtained some food from a farmer for her parents, who were in hiding with a family outside Leersum. The house was off the beaten track, at the top of a hill. As she did not want to run the risk of having a German confiscate her precious food, she had decided to walk through the woods instead of using the road.

She and I put all the parcels in the little cart and we thought that with two of us pulling it we should be able to get through the woods. Annie was in high spirits because someone had given her a few spoonfuls of salt in a small paper bag – there were no plastic bags in those days. She put this on top so that it would not be crushed by the other packages. She was really looking forward to the pleasant surprise she would give her mother, who, she knew, had no salt left.

All went well until we were almost there. Then the cart hit a concealed root of a tree and overturned. The little paper bag split and the salt spilled out, right into the tiniest puddle of water you could imagine! It was a real case of Murphy's law! Annie was disappointed but her mother was still overjoyed with the rest of the food, and delighted to see her daughter again too.

One day Paul Bos, who was the leader of the local Resistance action group and in charge of sabotage, was cycling through Driebergen, when the vicar stopped him.

'My spies tell me,' the vicar said, 'that Mr X is hoarding an awful lot of flour in his attic. We can't have that, with so many people starving. Can you do something about it?'

'I'll do my best, of course, vicar,' Paul replied with a roguish grin. 'It will be a pleasure to get the better of him seeing that he is pro-German.'

Paul talked to his group and several of them, together with a man from another action group who would not be recognised by the hoarder, went to the house. While the local men put on masks the stranger rang the doorbell. When the hoarder opened the door they all rushed in, overpowered him and tied his hands and legs up. The stranger stayed with him while the others removed the flour to a safe place. When this was done, he untied the hoarder's hands and made his escape while the man struggled to free his legs.

As the hoarder had a good bicycle and Paul's was in a bad state, Paul had taken the man's bike. He wasn't going to leave a pro-German with a good bicycle. He took the precaution, however, of changing the handlebar section and one of the wheels with those on his father's bicycle. It wouldn't do to run the risk of having the hoarder recognise his own bicycle somewhere.

A few days later Paul was talking to someone in the street and, to his surprise and discomfort, he saw the hoarder, who seemed to know the other man, coming towards them. The hoarder immediately started a long tirade about his trials and tribulations: not only had those criminals stolen his food but they had taken his bicycle as well. All the time he was standing next to what used to be, for most of its parts, his own bike. Mercifully, he never noticed!

Paul told the vicar the happy outcome of it all and it was agreed that the vicar would produce a list of the addresses of those people who needed the food most.

Betrayal in Maarn

On 14 February there was a crisis in Maarn. A black marketeer who had been caught stealing some cattle knew he would be given a stiff sentence, so he offered to name some members of the Resistance. In a small community it is difficult to do everything in total secret year after year. For instance, someone with a diver at home might tell someone else how he came by a ration card for him. Not everyone can hold his or her tongue. The temptation to tell a secret is ever present.

The black marketeer gave the names of Ted Visser and Bob Kröner. Both were arrested at their homes. That same morning Frans van Dijk, the leader of the Doorn Resistance, was due to have a meeting with Bob, but as he could not keep the appointment he asked his deputy Hein van Remmerden, to go instead.

When Hein rang the bell the maid came to the door, looking as white as a sheet. Immediately two Germans came round from the back of the house and asked what Hein wanted. He replied that he had met Mr Kröner in a pub, where they had played snooker. Hein had told him that he worked for the Germans at the fortification in Veenendaal. Kröner had asked him to take a small parcel to Veenendaal for him.

As he had papers to prove where he worked, the Germans believed him. His permit had to be initialled each day by the German in charge. Hein just added the signature and initialled it himself.

He left as quickly as he could and went to Ted's house to warn him, but the Germans were already there. This time he told the soldier who opened the door that he had tried to take a short cut to work and had got lost. He asked for directions. As his papers looked in order, the soldier told him how to return to the main road. He even went inside to ask the family if he had got the directions right.

Through the open door Hein saw Ted's in-laws, with whom he was staying, lying tied up on the floor. That morning Hein's path must really have been crossed by a black cat who gave him one of its nine lives!

Ted and his wife and Bob were taken to Utrecht. The in-laws were freed but were not allowed to go back into their house, which was sealed so that the Germans could search it thoroughly the next day. The family knew that a rifle, a pistol, ration cards and other incriminating items were kept in a hiding-place inside. If these were found it would mean a death sentence for them all. There was nothing against Ted yet, apart from the word of the black marketeer, though he had tried to make a run for it when they had left their house. He had been hampered by the leather coat he was wearing and, as bad luck would have it, the German who ran after him turned out to have been a champion sprinter.

Hein and Henny Idenburg, together with Henny's brother Cor, decided to burgle the house. They could not disturb the seals on the doors, of course, as that would have given the game away, but they were able to enter and leave through a window without appearing to have disturbed anything. The next day there was nothing incriminating left for the Germans to find, so at least the family was safe. Ted's wife was allowed to go home after a few days, but the Germans did not release Ted and Bob.

7

The Hunger-Winter

Acting on information received . . .

The longer the war went on, the more people were arrested. Although the Resistance members took every possible precaution, we could not work in total secrecy or in a vacuum. Inevitably, some of our comings and goings were bound to be observed in our locality, and there was always the risk that a Nazi would report his or her suspicions. The Germans were gradually obtaining enough information to break into our networks and were becoming more successful in finding our safe houses and arresting anyone they found there. It was a nerve-racking time for all of us. Besides, we were hungry and tired, too, on account of the constant strain day in and day out. Sometimes you had to steel yourself to carry on, but this was a roundabout you could not jump off once you were on it – not that we would have done while our country was not free.

I was staying in Veenendaal with Ab and Ger van 't Riet. Ab was the leader of the local LO (Assistance to Divers) group. He and Ger had two small sons, aged five and two. They were also giving shelter to two German Jewish divers. These were a married couple and the woman was often in a panic, which was understandable. She would say to me, 'Oh, Miss Elsa, don't go out today. I am so frightened. Please, Miss Elsa, stay inside. I am so scared.' And so on, endlessly. It was hard to bear when you were under strain yourself. She was also terribly worried about her husband's health. At every meal, Ger would serve the food and then the family would keep their eyes closed while grace was said. The diver took this opportunity to put some of her food on her husband's plate. I pretended not to see this.

On 21 November 1944 Ab went to take some ration cards to another member of the Resistance. While he was at the house the German security police (SD) arrived and both men were arrested.

I was told about it by George when I returned from my morning round. The Jewish couple had been taken to an emergency address and Ger was waiting anxiously for the Germans to come and search the house. She had got rid of anything incriminating, including a bag containing my belongings, which she had given to the person who had collected the divers. The Germans never came, inexplicably, but she was not to know that they wouldn't. Ab was sent to Neuengamme concentration camp, where he died in March 1945.

A new address was found for me with a baker. I was delighted to find my friend Ank Prevo there when I arrived. She was staying with the butcher next door. We were able to visit each other by going through the back gardens. It was a happy end to a disastrous day.

The next morning, when my alarm went off at 5.30 and I heard the rain beating against my window, I groaned to myself. I had to go on my usual round, another 50-km (31-mile) cycle ride along open roads with no shelter from the rain and wind. I was tired from the previous day's ride, my clothes had not dried out fully during the night and my shoes were still wet. There was, of course, no heating in the house at night and very little during the day. I heartily wished I could just turn over and go back to sleep.

When I emerged downstairs I found a slice of bread and margarine, with a small glass of off-white fluid that passed for milk, which my hostess had put out the night before. Everyone else was still asleep. I put on my coat and fetched my bicycle. It would still be pitch-dark for several hours and in the rain I had trouble staying on the dyke I had to follow for the first part of the journey.

That day everything went wrong and when I got home I was so depressed and exhausted that I felt I could not possibly go on doing this for much longer. And there, thank goodness, was Ank. She never made a fuss, and it was so good not to be alone at a time like that.

'What on earth has happened to you?' she asked. 'You look ghastly. I'll see if we have any milk I can heat up. Just sit and relax.'

A while later she returned with the drink, which I sipped gratefully. I told her about my day. 'It was simply awful. It never stopped raining – my shoes will never dry out again – and I got a flat tyre and had to walk almost an hour before I found someone who could fix it. That made me late and the girl I had to meet couldn't wait, so I had to go an extra 5 km (approx 3 miles) to find her and back again. Is this war never going to end?'

Ank was marvellous. 'Don't worry, you'll feel better in the morning. Why don't you ask the baker if he can put your shoes in his oven?

113

It might still be warm.'

I asked him and the oven did the trick. For as long as I stayed there I had dry shoes every morning. And Ank was right: I did feel better in the morning.

In February 1945 the Germans tried to arrest Oets (Klaas van Middelkoop), who was a branch manager of a bank in Driebergen. He saw them coming and just managed to disappear into the hiding place in his house, which was attached to the bank, in time. The house was searched but they did not find him. His bank clerk, who was a diver, ran off when he saw the German car stop outside; he did not wait long enough even to lock the safe.

When the Germans could not find Oets they took Ans, his wife. They punctiliously locked up the house, locked the bank safe, and then drove to the main branch of the bank to ask the manager if he knew where Oets was. The manager told them that, as far as he knew, the branch manager was working in Germany. They left the key to the safe with the manager and took Ans to the prison in Utrecht. She had some blank identity cards on her, but during the drive she contrived to push them into the seats of the car. In Utrecht she told the Germans that she did not know anything about her husband's alleged Resistance membership.

Each day Ans's father went to the prison to ask if he could take her home. After a week he decided that he would not go home without her. He told the Germans he already had one son working for them in Germany (he was a POW) and another in a mental hospital (he was a nurse) and now he was having to cope with his daughter's small child, who kept asking for his mother. Ans's father's desperate plea worked – the Germans had learned nothing from Ans anyway – and he was allowed to take her home. They travelled on his bicycle, with Ans sitting on the luggage rack.

Oets had not known when it would be safe for him to come out of his hiding place. Sometimes the Germans left someone in the house to catch people who emerged later. In this case, when it was safe Paul Bos went past the house whistling the tune of the basketball club. Luckily Oets could hear him and he came out and left the house. To show others that the address was no longer safe, Paul emptied a bottle of red ink over the pavement outside.

After the disaster at the De Jongs' in Langbroek, Harry Hello, the local Resistance leader, had left to stay in a neighbouring town. Sometimes he went back to Langbroek, to his parents' house, to meet other Resistance workers, most of whom had scattered and were now staying elsewhere.

One day Harry went home to meet Oets. Soon after Oets arrived, a warning came that in Cothen, a village 3 km (2 miles) away, two boys had been arrested. One of them belonged to the Resistance, but the other boy had just happened to call at the house. It was very sad because the Resistance boy had been betrayed by a relative who had fallen in love with a German and now believed all the Nazi doctrines. Her reward was 150 Dutch florins, the equivalent, at the rate of exchange at that time, of £12.50.

Harry decided to play safe and leave. He had a pre-arranged signal to show that there was danger about: his parents' neighbour would close the curtains in an upstairs room. Before ringing the bell at Harry's parents' house, a visitor would look up at the window next door.

It was not long before the Germans arrived. The family had long since taken the precaution of leaving their photograph albums with a friend. The Germans asked for Harry's photo after they had searched the house. His father was very helpful. 'Of course,' he said, 'we have a very nice photo of him.' He brought one of Harry as a baby in his mother's arms. They asked for a description. When it came to the colour of Harry's hair, his father said, 'Not black, but definitely not fair either. Not very light, but I wouldn't call it brown.' Asked about height and weight, he replied, 'Not very tall, but I would not call him small. Not really fat, but not thin either.'

The Germans gave up, but they took away Harry's brother-in-law, who happened to be there. Then they went to the local church, which they searched. It was shortly before the service was due to begin – because of the curfew, evensong took place in the afternoon. The minister decided to let them do what they wanted and he started the service while the Germans searched the vestry. The divers who had come to attend the service (Langbroek was so remote that it was usually safe for them to go to church) had quickly left once word had been passed around that the Germans were at the house. The soldiers found a few radios but not the weapons they had hoped to seize. Those were hidden in a family tomb that was no longer in use. The minister naturally denied any knowledge of how the radios had found their way into his vestry.

Harry's brother-in-law was questioned, but they could see from his papers that he did not live in Langbroek. They showed him photographs, among them one of Oets, which they had taken from Oets's house. Although he had seen Oets only a short time ago he denied ever having seen him. The Germans let him go.

The search for Resistance members went on relentlessly. On 28 February Frans van Dijk, who led the Doorn Resistance, was arrested. He was never interrogated, however. On 8 March he was one of the total of 263 members of the Resistance, imprisoned in different places, who were to be executed as a reprisal for the attack on General Rauter (see page 102). Some were taken from the prison at Utrecht and executed at Fort De Bilt, not far away. Ted Visser and Bob Kröner were among them, as were the two boys from Cothen. People across the whole region were shattered.

The Doorn undertaker promised Frans's family that he would bring him home. This was not easy. The undertaker borrowed a horse and cart and drove the 20 km (12 miles) to the Fort. It took a long time to obtain permission to take the body. Frans had been the town treasurer and everyone there knew him. The Germans usually sent an observer to a funeral in a case like that. They wanted to know who was coming and what was being said. No member of the Resistance could risk attending. Frans's brother gave the address. That was not easy to do either. It was not possible to say anything negative about the Germans – there was no point in being arrested too. What was said had to be more indirect. The Germans had not banned the Bible. Hitler liked to refer in his speeches to 'Providence' and the Wehrmacht had the words 'God with us' on their belts. So Frans's brother was able to quote from the Bible, saying, 'We all remember the words of the psalmist: "I will keep my mouth with a bridle, while the wicked is before me. I was dumb with silence, I held my peace, even from good; and my sorrow was stirred." (Psalm 39, 1–2)

Then he paraphrased the Lord's Prayer, with suitable texts in between the different lines. When he reached "Forgive us our trespasses as we forgive those who trespass against us", he added 'The psalmist says: "Do not I hate them, O Lord, that hate thee? I hate them with perfect hatred" (Psalm 139, 21–22). After the funeral the German observer looked at all the flowers, but as the family had taken off the cards he was none the wiser.

One Sunday the Germans went through the streets of Veenendaal announcing through a loudhailer that an airborne attack was expected and nobody was to go out. If they did, they risked being shot. Most of the Resistance members were able to leave the town in case it was a ruse to enable the Germans to search the houses, but nothing happened. Shortly afterwards, on 2 March, the same announcement was made. It seemed safer to stay at home than to risk being

Harry Hello, 1920-1987   Frans van Dijk, 1904-1945

Ted Visser, 1918-1945

Zonhof, 1945

Bob Kröner, 1904–1945

shot outside. This time, however, the Germans went to all the addresses where they knew that Resistance members had ever been. They arrested several people, among them George, the leader of the Veenendaal group. They also picked up a few people who had either not heard the announcement or had risked being out nevertheless. The two groups of prisoners were held in one large room. George contrived to switch groups, so that he was with those who had been out of doors. Late in the afternoon that group was released.

One tragedy that arose from these events occurred when the father of a little girl who had diphtheria had gone out to fetch a doctor. After his arrest he was taken to an office where he was given a permit to go to the surgery, but it all took so long that the child had suffocated before the doctor could be summoned.

Those who were arrested indoors on that day were people who had been betrayed by the Veenendaal man arrested earlier for riding a motor cycle without the proper papers. Luckily for me, he did not know where I was. The only person who knew that was George, who decided that Veenendaal was becoming too hot for him – he could not risk being recognised and re-arrested – so he left to stay with a family in Leersum. We decided that I could stay on in Veenendaal as apparently the Germans did not know my address. Moreover, no one local knew it, so I could not be betrayed.

Some time later I was given a matchbox to take to an address outside Leersum. There was less than an hour and a half to go before curfew time. I would have to hurry, as the trip would take a good hour. Beneath the matches was a microfilm with the secret code being used by the German division stationed in the region. I borrowed a packet with three cigarettes in it to give me a reason for having the matchbox. Cigarettes were very hard to come by and were worth a lot on the black market.

A short distance from my destination I was stopped by two Germans. They were standing just round a bend in the road and I had not seen them, so they startled me. They asked me where I was going and pointed out that I was a long way from Veenendaal itself, where my papers said I lived, with the curfew due to start in half an hour. My story, that I was going to visit a patient, seemed to convince them, but they insisted on searching my bag. They took everything out, looked at the cigarettes, decided not to take them, and then one of them had the matchbox in his hands. I held my breath and tried not to look tense. It did not apparently occur to him to take the matches out. After a pause they handed everything back and said I

117

could go. I made an effort not to show any reaction that might make them suspicious again as I remounted my bike, but I was really shaking like a leaf. I had never been so terrified.

Ten minutes later I was at my contact's house. An agent was waiting to take the film to the Allies that same night. He was evidently going to risk breaking the curfew. The people at the house put me up for the night.

A week later the owner of the house was arrested and kept in prison until the end of the war. That was another safe address lost. It went on like that all the time. In Langbroek the only contact left was Kees ten Wolde, and he had some very high-ranking officers billeted on him, so it would have been too risky to go there except as a last resort.

About a fortnight after the arrests in Veenendaal I had to cycle to Leersum. On my way there I met a fifteen-year-old boy pushing what looked like an old man in a wheelbarrow. It was a moment before I recognised them. The man looked thirty years older than he really was. He had a bicycle shop in Veenendaal and in the autumn of 1944 the Resistance had had its headquarters upstairs. As there were always people calling at the shop for cycle repairs, Resistance members could go there too without attracting attention.

The man had been arrested on the same day that all the other arrests had been made in the town. He told me that he had been questioned about me several times. Although he had in fact seen me daily that autumn he had denied ever having met me. He warned me now to be very wary. The Germans definitely had my description.

He had been ill with a stomach ulcer which had started bleeding after he had been in prison for ten days. The prison doctor had thought he was dying, so he was allowed to go. His son had called at the prison to ask about him and when he was told he could take him home he had borrowed a wheelbarrow and was now trundling there with him – a distance of 65 km (40 miles)! After hearing his account, I realised that the Germans were seriously on my trail in Veenendaal. I decided it was time for me to move again.

It was now the end of March. It was arranged that I would stay in Leersum with the Post family, who were themselves evacuees from Scheveningen. I could pretend to be a 'niece'. They lived in 'Zonhof', a former boarding house, which had a central corridor with two rooms on each side. This turned out to be the perfect place to hide, though we certainly had our moments there.

I meet the SS

Soon after I settled in at the house I went deep into the woods with George for target practice with a new handgun. We pinned an envelope on a tree and I had to try to hit it. Afterwards I took the gun back with me.

When I walked through the door of Zonhof I almost bumped into an SS officer. He startled me, and I immediately assumed he was there to arrest me. What flashed through my mind was that my only chance was to make a run for it. I put my hand in my coat pocket to pull out the gun.

At that moment he said in a very friendly tone, 'Hello, you must be the niece. We have taken over the rooms on this side of the corridor, but we have allowed your aunt and her family to keep the other rooms.'

Phew! Thank heavens I had hesitated for a split second before doing something irreparable! I smiled weakly, still clutching the gun in my pocket, inclined my head by way of acknowledgement and walked past him. My heart was pounding fit to burst.

The German turned out to be a lieutenant-colonel, and he had moved in, together with a sergeant and another soldier who acted as his driver. This I thought, was going to be interesting, to say the least. Would I be recognised when they had a closer look?

When he was drunk the colonel let slip that he worked for the Gestapo in Utrecht. As the fighting came closer he and his men went to work in the morning and came back in the afternoon. They were too scared of being bombed to stay in Utrecht at night when the bombers flew over.

George told me to be as friendly as possible with them, as I might be able to find out something of their plans. This was quite an experience for me, to be so close to real Nazis. I had very mixed feelings about it. I hated the Nazis fiercely. They had killed some of my closest friends, burnt down their homes and generally behaved despicably. I could scarcely bear to think of being under the same roof. On the other hand, if I could find out what they were doing it would obviously help the Resistance and might save lives. I was also, I must admit, pretty scared that one day they might see a description of me at their headquarters and recognise me. Well, I didn't have much choice anyway, as I had nowhere else to go to at the time, so I thought I had better do as George had asked.

Nel Post, whose husband was on the run after he had escaped from arrest, lived in the house with her four children. She, of course played a part in what George wanted done. In the evenings Nel invited the Germans to join the family. The men much appreciated this, as not all Dutch people were so friendly. The Germans still had a good supply of schnapps and they imbibed freely. One night they were so drunk they showed us the precautions they had taken in case they had to take flight suddenly. The heels of the colonel's boots were hollow and could be unscrewed. They were filled with gold.

On the evening that the Germans heard on their radio that the Russians were entering Berlin, the men drowned their sorrows more than ever. The colonel gave a toast and said, 'Berlin is no longer ours. It was German Berlin and now it is Russian Berlin. Let's drink to Russian Berlin.' By the time they passed out, the rest of us had gone to bed. Our bedrooms were upstairs and, thank goodness, the Germans had their rooms downstairs.

When Hitler handed over command to Admiral Dönitz it was difficult to explain this to the troops. Their officers decided to give all the soldiers in the village a litre (2 pints) of schnapps. The alcohol was brought to Zonhof in milk churns from the dairy, which was no longer in operation as there was no more milk – the Germans had taken almost all our cows and other farm animals. The drink was measured out in the kitchen at Zonhof. Every soldier who brought empty bottles received a ration.

A few hours later there were soldiers lying everywhere in the streets, dead drunk. One man drove his motor cycle through the front door of the house and into the kitchen, while another came in on his horse and rode round the table. It was a sight to behold! We quietly got on with clearing up the mess as best we could, with only cold water and no soap. Our tolerance resulted in much goodwill for the family, however, which came in useful soon afterwards.

The men who were billeted in our house were also dead drunk that night. I was just going to sleep, when I heard shouting downstairs. I sat up to listen better. They were saying, 'Where is that girl? We want that girl.' The Germans had taken over so many rooms that I was sleeping in the attic, and the door did not lock. In a flash I was out of bed and running to the nearest bedroom, which was that of Dick Post, Nel's eleven-year-old son. His door did not lock either, but Dick helped me to barricade ourselves in, using a table. The Germans started to push at the door, so we piled the chairs on top of the table and pushed back as hard as we could. The door held and eventually we heard them stumbling off downstairs. I did not dare go back to bed that night, so I sat in a chair in Dick's room.

A few days later the German Green Police (so called because their uniform was green) arrived and searched the house. They said there were partisans there. George was visiting us at the time and he and I were both put up against a wall with our hands up. We thought this was going to be the end for us. It was certainly a frightening experience. I was on tenterhooks, wondering what would happen to us. Then we had a stroke of luck – the colonel came home early. He wanted to know what was happening. After listening to the police he said, 'I know these people. I live here. They are my friends. It is nonsense to think that they have anything to do with the Resistance. They are on our side.' And he kicked the police out.

In Germany there was a very strict hierarchy. The SS was senior to the Green Police, and of course the colonel was the highest in rank of those present. So the SS probably saved George's and my life. How long would our luck hold? I wondered. What had brought the Green Police to the house in the first place? Would they be watching the house and following me when I went out? It was nerve-racking not knowing exactly how much they knew.

In the grip of winter

As the front came closer, the part of the country that was still occupied became smaller. There were, therefore, proportionally more Germans among us. They became nastier and nastier as their military position became less secure. They all wanted our bicycles now and would stop us in the street and take them. They started to come into our houses and took our blankets, or our food if they saw us with any. They forbade us to cut down trees for firewood.

As far back as 9 October 1944, the electricity company in the Province of Utrecht had stopped supplying households with electricity and on 25 October the gasworks had followed suit. That left us with only wood or coal to burn, if we had any, but long before the winter was over supplies of those had run out. It was so cold that if you took a glass of water to bed it had frozen solid by the morning.

My parents took advantage of the fact that the local Wehrmacht commander lived in the road behind our house. He naturally had an electricity supply, which meant that all the houses on his side of the road as far as the next corner also had electricity. The neighbours directly behind our house were among the lucky ones. In order to poach the Germans' electricity, my parents ran a long lead (the gardens were 25 metres/27.5 yards each, so it took some 50 metres/ 55 yards of flex, made up of bits and pieces) from the neighbour's house to ours. Ank tied rags round all the many connections to insulate them and prevent them from becoming separated. Neighbours in our street came in the evening (via the back gardens because of the curfew) to do their mending and sewing by the light of the single lamp that the one flex permitted. It was better than nothing, and everyone enjoyed the joke against the Wehrmacht commander.

How to obtain wood was a major preoccupation that winter. The schools had been closed, so the children helped to do the jobs their fathers would have done if they had not been in hiding, or working as slave labour in Germany, as so many of them were. If the Germans took the wood you had gathered, that was bad enough. It was even worse if they took your axe as well. That was a disaster, as you could not buy a replacement. Not everyone had owned an axe before the war and if you needed to borrow one you had to take great care of it. People took turns to keep watch for Germans while others hacked down small trees as quickly as they could.

That winter over 22,000 people died of starvation. With no more food reaching the population the churches got together to collect food from the farms in the east, where there was still some. This needed a special permit from the Germans. In most places only inhabitants who had lost more than a third of their body weight (which had to be certified by a doctor) were entitled to extra food collected by the churches. In December 1944 rations had been reduced from 950 to 700 calories per day. In January they went down again, to 600 calories, and then, in February, to 500 calories. Even if you had a ration card you could not always buy the food you were entitled to. If shops did not have the produce, the coupon was cancelled. The Germans would not allow food to be transported westwards in quantity because of the Dutch railway strike. They put up posters showing a railway line, a skull and cross-bones and the word 'strike'. The message was that it was our own fault if we were starving. The Germans did not mention that they had taken, and were continuing to take our food to Germany.

We were fortunate that my father was an enterprising man. He bought three beehives early in the war and these provided us with a precious substitute for sugar. In the final years of the war the heather must have been particularly good, for the bees produced an abundance of honey then. The family never had the luxury of putting it on bread but it was a great asset for bartering at a time when everyone was starving.

My father knew nothing about bee-keeping and had to learn from scratch – or should I say from sting. He wore a protective hood but inevitably he was still stung. It takes a while for a keeper to become immune to bee stings and poor father had plenty of them. One day he counted as many as fifty. On this occasion his leg seemed to have been the target and it swelled up so much that he could not walk or put on his shoe. It so happened that he was due to accompany my mother to her brother's funeral the next day, but he was unable to go, and I went instead. This was the silliest excuse I had ever heard for not attending a funeral, but my mother was sad all the same.

We also had two apple trees and a plum tree in the garden. One apple tree gave a good harvest of fruit but the other did not. The whole garden was turned over to growing vegetables, including the lawns at the front and back of the house. We preserved as much of the produce as we could for the winter.

Another way of obtaining food was to search for potatoes after the farmers had finished lifting them. Ank would go out with a hand-fork and root about in the earth. Sometimes a potato had been left in the ground and if she persevered for hours and hours she might be able to half-fill a bucket, which she would return with in triumph.

As for cooking we had all sorts of devices to save fuel – at first gas, when it was still available, and later wood. We used a hay-box, whereby you cook something for a short time in the normal way and then put it in a box lined with hay or straw. This heats up and eventually completes the cooking. Patience certainly became a virtue in those days.

The churches in Driebergen sent a delegation to the local Wehrmacht commander, who was not a Nazi. He gave them a permit to buy food east of the river IJssel, on behalf of the churches. My father knew some of the farmers there and he agreed to organise the purchase of supplies. As he was forty-nine years old then, he was just within the age group of men who had to work for the Germans. He had been exempted because he was a headmaster, but now that the schools were closed it was risky to rely on his exemption. A clerk in the council offices changed my father's year of birth from 1895 to 1893 and all was well.

On 27 December 1944 he went with my teenage sister Ank and two women to find farmers who were willing to sell food. They arranged that the bulk of their purchases would be fetched later by young men on carrier-tricycles who would be given special permits by the Germans. His party took with them what they could carry on their bicycles. This expedition of my father's took so long that on the way back they were still 16 km (10 miles) from home when the curfew started. They went to the local Wehrmacht commander (a different one this time) to ask permission to continue their journey, but he refused to allow it. Fortunately they found shelter in a house belonging to the Red Cross, but it was freezing cold in there as the house had never been heated. They found some straw inside, but that was all, and they had to huddle together to try to keep even slightly warm. It was a bitterly cold night.

Before he had set out on the return trip my father had been given a chicken by one of the farmers. He had cycled for over 130 km (80 miles) through the snow and freezing cold with this chicken. Then, only 4 km (2.4 miles) from home, a German stopped him and took the bird. Father was both disappointed and annoyed, of course, but these things happened all the time. It was even worse for people who had bartered their family heirlooms for food and then had it taken from them.

I decided to go with my father and his little group on his next foray in January. An extra cyclist could bring back more food. I told my Resistance friends when I would be back and it looked as though it ought to be a smooth trip. On the return journey, however, my bicycle broke down. It took hours to find someone who knew someone who could deal with it. When it was fixed, we decided to take a short cut to make up time. This involved cycling through the National Park, 'De Hoge Veluwe', a deer sanctuary of some 5.500 hectares (13.600 acres) in size and consisting mainly of heathland and forests. A snowplough had made a path through it, but cycling was still difficult and we regularly fell off. What kept us going was the knowledge that we had so much food with us. Half-way through, however, one of the women fell off and found she could not remount. Her cycle was too heavily loaded and the path too slippery. We walked a couple of miles, pushing our bikes, but that took a long time. My father advised me to go on alone. If we had to walk all the way we would not arrive back until the next day. If I failed to return when I had said I would, the members of our action group would assume I had been arrested and they would all have to go and find other safe houses, which, alas, was becoming difficult – there were not many left. There was nothing for it: I had to meet my deadline. It was not very pleasant cycling alone. Although I was used to it in our own area, on this occasion, much farther afield, I missed my companions. We had been cheering each other up all the time, and keeping each other going. There were no more mishaps, though, and I arrived back safely in the afternoon. My father and the others arrived some three hours later, just before curfew. They had walked for another two hours and then had found better roads so that they could cycle again. I could have stayed with them after all – but we didn't know that at the time and you can't always make the right decision. At least we were able to deliver the food, and the load I had carried was a bonus.

I go to the front line

On 20 April 1945 a BI agent arrived at the house of Kees van Dijk in Leersum to ask for a guide to take him through the lines with some urgent and important documents. The agent had identity papers that described him as a doctor and he carried a stethoscope in an outside pocket. Kees asked me to go because, with me as a nurse, we could concoct a cover story about visiting a farmer's wife who was going to have a baby. I did not wear my nurse's uniform on this occasion because, being tight and long, it would have hampered me in climbing over the barbed wire. If we were stopped, I had my nurse's papers and I could say that my only uniform was being laundered – we had no clothing coupons for uniforms, so it was credible to have only one outfit.

I tucked the documents securely inside the top of my dress and we set off. It seemed a good omen that that day was Hitler's birthday. The first part of the journey was not too difficult. We went through the fields and over some deserted German fortifications. Then we were stopped at a German command post – the position of these changed very frequently, so I could not guarantee to avoid all of them. Our story held up because we could point to a farm in the distance as our destination. Once we were out of sight of the Germans, we changed direction and warily approached the front line.

There was barbed wire just about everywhere and getting across it was no joke. I climbed over first and then the agent lifted the bicycles over to me before he followed. It was a slow business, trying to avoid tearing our clothes or scratching our hands and legs, or damaging our bikes. We thought we must be nearly in no-man's-land, when without warning the Canadians started shelling the area. We just managed to fling ourselves into a ditch and lie flat. Where I had landed, the ditch was overgrown with nettles. Later on I realised my legs, arms and hands were covered in red blotches from their sting, but at the time I was too frightened to notice. Less than 20 metres/22 yards away a cow was killed. Every now and then the agent would shout to me: 'Are you still alive?' I doubt if he could hear my answer above the almost constant din. The whining of the shells and the crump of the explosions were deafening and unnerving for a girl who had never experienced a battlefield bombardment before. I was nearly scared out of my wits. This battering lasted for about half an hour and then it stopped as suddenly as it had started.

We looked around cautiously, scrambled to our feet, dusted ourselves down – the ditch had done nothing for my clothes, which I always tried so hard to keep clean – reassured each other briefly that we were unhurt and set off again. Eventually we reached a farm that happened to have been a contact address for the Resistance when we were still in Veenendaal. This was now in an area that the Germans had abandoned, so the agent was able to cycle the last couple of miles to the Canadians unhindered. The farmer's son promised to act as his guide.

I decided to go back, as there was still a lot of work to be done in and around Leersum. The farmer gave me some milk, so that if the Germans stopped me I could say I had gone to fetch it from a farm. I would be pleased to drink it later, too. My return journey was much harder because now there was nobody to hand my bicycle over the wire to me. I counted thirteen barbed-wire obstacles I had to negotiate in all. I avoided damaging the bike, but at the penultimate obstacle I fell and tore my dress so badly that it was completely ruined.

A few days after this adventure, on a separate mission, I was still a half-hour's bike ride away from Leersum and it was almost curfew time. I was so tired, having cycled all day and being very hungry, that I just had to dismount. I was exhausted. As I stood there, two Germans came along with a horse and cart and they stopped to ask me if I wanted a lift. Since I had nothing incriminating on me, I decided to accept their offer. I could really not have cycled any farther. I was completely worn out. The Germans took me right into Leersum – I was careful, though, not to let them stop anywhere near the house where I was actually staying. I staggered indoors, collapsed on my bed and fell asleep the instant my head touched the pillow.

Hardship

Life in Leersum towards the end of the war became very difficult. The waterworks stopped providing water. Zonhof had its own bore hole, as had a number of houses, so we were all right. Other householders had to go to the dairy every morning between 8 and 9 a.m. to fetch water. The milk churns were now filled with water and daily rations were given out. Curfew was imposed from 9 a.m. until 8 a.m. the next day, so there was a great rush of people to get to the dairy and back in time. The front line was so close now that the Germans did not want civilians in the streets. It was sheer bullying. We could not go out to try to barter for food or to collect wood. Some people philosophically played bridge for hours on end. Our days became unbearable, especially as we hoped that each one would be the last before we were liberated – but it didn't happen. It was terribly frustrating, and we were all tensed up.

Persistent to the end

Despite the fact that the Germans must have known that their time was almost up, they continued to hunt for Resistance workers. On 2 May several members of the Resistance in Doorn were arrested, including the leader, Hein van Remmerden. They were badly beaten up, bound like sausages, and thrown into an open truck. Hein was interrogated by the Gestapo in Zeist. They wanted to know where the Resistance had hidden its weapons. Every time Hein said he could not understand German he was beaten again. They gave him only one small piece of bread to eat each day. As he was kept handcuffed, he had to manoeuvre this between his knees before he could eat it. On 5 May, the day after the Germans had surrendered, the Gestapo officer admitted to Hein that they had lost the war. He told Hein he respected him for holding out under interrogation and asked him to shake hands.

Hein asked him, 'As what?'

'You decide,' said the German.

So Hein said, 'As a very bitter enemy with his enemy.'

This was solemnly agreed upon.

It was now 5 May, Liberation Day. The men from Doorn were taken to Utrecht and the car stopped at Fort De Bilt, the place where executions took place. Their lives were now held by a thread. They waited anxiously for over an hour. Apparently the Germans had wanted to execute them but knew that they could be severely punished if they did, because the war was now over. During the surrender talks they had been told that in no circumstances should there be any more executions. The Germans must have been debating the issue all the time the prisoners were kept waiting in the car. Eventually they were driven to the prison. They were given no food, but at least they were not interrogated again. One of the men had a small window in his cell and he could see a Dutch flag flying, so he knew that liberation had come at last. The next day, 6 May, the Canadians came to the prison and freed everyone. We were all overjoyed at this outcome.

127

8

Liberation?

Introduction

On 16 April 1945 the 2nd Canadian Army Corps completed the liberation of the northern and eastern parts of the Netherlands. This left the densely populated Provinces of North Holland, South Holland and Utrecht, with 4.5 million inhabitants, still occupied by 120,000 German soldiers, many of them fanatical SS men.

The next day the Germans blew up the dykes of the Wieringermeerpolder – an area close to where the IJsselmeer joins the North Sea, near the tip of the peninsula on which Amsterdam, well to the south, stands. All the farmland that had been reclaimed there from the sea was flooded. The water came up to the roofs of the farm buildings and destroyed the results of many years of hard work. They said they did it to prevent Allied airborne landings, but they could have opened the locks in a controlled way and achieved their purpose without doing all that wanton damage to our hard-won land.

Field-Marshal Montgomery now called a halt to the advance of his forces. The Canadians stopped only some 16 km (10 miles) short of Leersum. Montgomery knew that if fighting were to continue there would be a great many casualties, both military and civilian, especially in the big cities. Besides, the civilians were starving and their plight was desperate. Something had to be done on humanitarian grounds.

The Allies decided to hold talks with the Germans. These began on 30 April, but the day before this they started 'Operation Manna'. Between 29 April and 8 May the British and Americans made 5,568 flights to drop food over the western part of the Netherlands, 3,610 of them while the country was still occupied. Everyone who could helped to gather up the packages. Some 4,000 people went out to do this daily. In some places those who helped were searched before they returned home, to make sure they had not kept any of the food for themselves. This was a harsh imposition when everyone was so hungry, but it was essential that the apportionment was seen to be scrupulously fair.

Distribution was difficult. The Dutch had no public transport or private cars, few horses or even bicycles by now, since the Germans had taken a great number of them. Besides, many of the packages had burst open when they hit the ground. Flour was mixed with sand or mud. Some supplies had landed in water. Everything had to be cleaned up and some of it repacked. It was not until 7 May that we each received on our ration card 400 grammes of bread (half a loaf), 100 grammes (4 oz) of margarine or butter, 50 grammes (2 oz) of cocoa, and the choice between a tin of bacon, cheese, sausage or egg powder. On 13 May, more than a week after liberation, rations went up to 1,800 calories a day – still not enough, but we were no longer actually starving.

There was one particularly sad consequence of the Allied action. The planes had flown in very low at only 100–200 metres (330–660 feet) and on 7 May, three days after the Germans had officially surrendered, some German fanatics fired an anti-aircraft gun and shot down one of the American Flying Fortresses as it was crossing the coast on its return home. It crashed into the North Sea and only two out of a crew of thirteen were rescued.

The Germans went on with senseless killing for some time. On the same day, when the people of Amsterdam were out celebrating and a large crowd had gathered in the square in front of the Royal Palace to greet the British troops, Germans suddenly started shooting into the crowd. They killed twenty-two people and severely wounded another sixty. It seemed that madness or sheer evil had taken over at that moment.

Meanwhile the official talks were held between the American General Bedell Smith, Prince Bernhard and Seyss-Inquart. Bedell Smith advised Seyss-Inquart to surrender and stop the war, but the Austrian Nazi refused, saying that history would judge him badly if he did. Bedell Smith retorted impatiently, 'You may as well give in. You will be hanged anyway.' Unimpressed by that argument, Seyss-Inquart replied. 'That leaves me cold.' To which the American responded, 'It will.'

On 4 May the decision was taken out of Seyss-Inquart's hands when the Germans surrendered formally to Montgomery all their troops throughout north-western Europe, including, of course, those in the Netherlands. That evening at a quarter to nine the surrender was announced in a radio broadcast from the liberated south. Many people still had hidden radios, so the news soon spread. The curfew was still in being but word was passed along through the back gardens. Everyone expected the Canadians to arrive early the next morning – they were so near. We could scarcely bear the suspense.

The SS go on the rampage

The Resistance had been busy for weeks making lists of Nazis to be arrested. The command of the BS issued a flood of orders about what to do and how to act. Early on 5 May George came to Zonhof and asked me to go to Veenendaal with all these orders and give them to the local BS commander there. Even though we were all feeling a little dizzy with everything that was happening, and we could so easily have let down our guard, some sixth sense warned me still to be careful. So I put on my nurse's uniform and took my forged identity card and permits with me, hiding the BS papers under my clothes.

When I arrived at the outskirts of Veenendaal, instead of seeing the first Canadian patrol, as I had hoped, I was stopped by an SS man with a sub-machine-gun. He wanted to know what I was doing outside. Since 17 April the local inhabitants had been allowed out only between 10 and 11 a.m. to fetch water. As usual, doctors, nurses, midwives and clerks working in the council offices were exempt, but it was just as well that I could show the proper permits and say I was on my way to visit a patient.

At the Resistance headquarters my friends had been celebrating all night. Someone had kept a few bottles for the occasion and they were still in party mood when I arrived. After I gave them the new orders I warned them to be careful, telling them how I had been challenged on the way there. The SS evidently had not given up yet.

I did not want to risk returning the same way, so we worked out a route which went mainly via back alleys and across fields, so that I could leave the town without using the roads. I was uneasy all the way back – I couldn't say why – and I decided as I approached Leersum to use my old route through the forest. Just before I turned off into the trees I thought I heard some shooting, but now that the Germans had officially surrendered I told myself I was imagining things.

As I came out of the forest and approached the outskirts of Leersum I heard some shots that sounded very close – close enough for me to leap off my bike and throw myself flat on the ground. I stayed there, keeping perfectly still, for what seemed like a very long time, not daring to raise my head to look around me. Hearing nothing more, I eventually got up very cautiously. There was no one about. I decided not to go right into Leersum. Mrs Loudon's house was closer, I thought it would be safer to go there.

I stayed with Mrs Loudon for a couple of hours, during which time everything remained quiet. We talked together about our hopes for the future, now that the war was over and the Germans would be leaving our country. I would have to complete my school-leaving examinations, for my studies had been brought to a sudden end. It would also be marvellous to be able to go home to my parents' house and to sleep peacefully in my own bed again. We were both full of dreams about what we would eat when we could lay our hands on plenty of food, and how good it would be to be able to renew our wardrobes and buy new shoes. Then I set off for Zonhof, hoping not to run into any trouble. I arrived safely, and reported to George, who was waiting anxiously for me, as I had been away longer then I had intended.

Now I found out what the shooting had been about. The local BS commander in Leersum had ordered his men to a meeting at 9 a.m. to discuss plans. The venue was the old MOVA brick factory on the outskirts of the village. The men were told to come in small groups of two or three and to carry their weapons discreetly concealed. This was not easy to do if you had a Sten gun or rifle, so the men put them in sacks over their shoulders. As bad luck would have it, at 8.30 a.m. five men were on their way to the MOVA when they encountered three SS men.

'Come with us,' said one arrogantly. 'We need you to peel our potatoes.'

'What is in those sacks?' asked another.

'Axes,' a Resistance man replied. 'We are going to gather firewood.'

This was a risky admission, because the Germans had earlier forbidden us to chop down any more trees, but in the circumstances it seemed better to say that if it would stop the Germans from looking in the sacks.

'Show me your identity card,' an SS man commanded.

'Oh dear, I seem to have left it at home,' the Resistance man countered. 'I'll go and fetch it.'

When he turned to go, one of the SS pointed his pistol at him so he had to stay where he was.

Then one of the Germans opened a sack and saw the weapons.

'Partisans!' he shouted.

Two of the Resistance men on the edge of the group made a run

131

for it before the Germans could react, and they escaped, but the other three were arrested.

While they were being marched off, they gave each other a sign and simultaneously attacked the three SS men, each man jumping on one German. This seemed their best chance of escape, as only one SS man was apparently armed, with a pistol.

This man, as he rolled on the ground, managed to hit his assailant with the pistol. One of the other Dutchmen saw this and he grabbed his sack, which contained a rifle, and fired through the sacking, killing the SS man. The second SS man ran off and the third one was captured and marched off to the MOVA, where the Resistance men fully expected to see their leader.

Two days earlier, however, about fifty members of the Luftwaffe had taken over the MOVA. As no civilians had been allowed outside for the past week, the local people did not know about this. The Resistance men approached with their prisoner and they were horrified suddenly to see all these Germans swarming all over the place. They abandoned their prisoner and just managed to disperse and disappear in time.

At the same time, other members of the Resistance were on their way to the rendezvous. The brothers Kees and Jan van Dijk were stopped, searched, arrested, and taken to the MOVA. Wim Selles, a teacher whose home was near Arnhem, where he had belonged to the LO, had been evacuated to Leersum after the battle and had joined the local BS. That morning he had arranged to go with Gerrit Storm to the meeting. His house was almost opposite the MOVA, at the end of a 200-metre (220-yard) driveway, but because of a bend in the drive the two men could not see the MOVA itself. They walked a short distance along the road and heard shooting. Taking cover behind a spruce tree, they spotted SS men only about 60 metres (65 yards) in front of them.

Gerrit Storm was an army officer. His training had taught him to stay in the open if caught in a situation like that. He decided to crawl back and try to get away across the fields to Amerongen. He was lucky enough to meet two poachers on the way. They knew every tree and bush in the area and gave him directions. Wim Selles, however, had decided not to go with Gerrit Storm. He did not want to leave his wife and six children and, after all, he was only a stone's throw from home. He was unarmed, so he had nothing to hide. He started to walk back – but he never arrived. He was stopped in his driveway and taken to join the Van Dijk brothers.

Wim Selles, 1910-1945

Kees van Dijk, 1909-1945

Jan van Dijk, 1921-1945

Air Forces Escape and Evasion Society Memorial Plaque

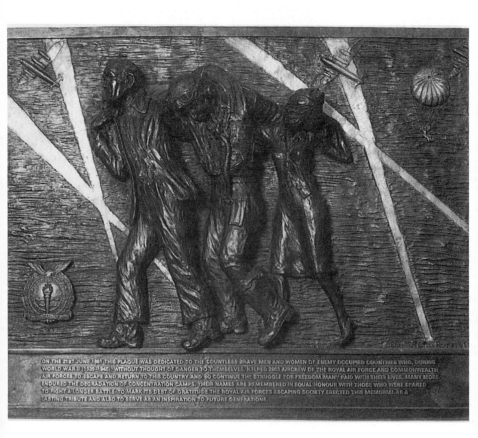

Memorial plaque in St. Clement Danes, London
to commemorate the helpers who lost their lives

Meanwhile the SS man who had escaped the earlier encounter with Resistance men had told his story to his commanding officer at his headquarters in the Lomboklaan in Leersum. The CO went to the MOVA and ordered the immediate execution of Kees, Jan and Wim. These must have been the shots I had heard earlier. Their bodies were dumped by the roadside.

In the Lomboklaan in Leersum the SS had requisitioned three houses, one for use as an armoury and store, one as a kitchen, and one – called 'De Stroohoed' because it had a thatched roof – for the administration. The SS now ran through the streets arresting anyone who was outside and took them to De Stroohoed. Among those taken there was a Jewish man who had been hiding in Leersum but, growing impatient, had gone out to look for the Canadians. He was severely beaten up. The SS searched houses in the village and started looting.

Three more Resistance members on their way to the MOVA walked into the Lomboklaan without knowing what was going on. They were stopped, of course, and one of them was asked to open his rucksack. When the SS saw weapons, they shot him on the spot. The other men tried to run off, but they were also killed. Three prisoners were ordered to move the bodies to the side of the road. They were not allowed to carry them reverently but had to drag them along the ground. Road-blocks were set up round the village and anyone who tried to enter Leersum was arrested and taken to a small field. You can imagine the terror they felt, as they fully expected to be shot there. If I had not heeded my 'sixth sense' and had tried to go straight back to Zonhof I would have been taken to that field too.

Early in the afternoon some of us in the Resistance who were still free gathered together in a shed behind Jan Lagemaat's house. Nobody knew exactly what had happened that morning to cause all this commotion in the village. George asked me to go and find out what I could, since it was not safe for any of the men to do this.

After my experiences earlier that morning I was very nervous about going out, but I realised that we had to know what was happening. Luckily, I noticed that the soldier-driver who was billeted on us at Zonhof, opposite Jan's house, had returned. He was a Czech, very anti-Nazi, who had been forced to join the German army. He had told me this one evening when the officers had been too drunk to hear what he said. As Nel Post's older son, who was eighteen, had gone out in the morning and not returned, that gave me an excuse for wanting to go out myself to see what had happened to my 'cousin'. I asked the soldier to come with me, and he agreed. He behaved very correctly and I felt I could believe his story about being a Czech and not a Nazi. With him as escort, I was relatively safe from molestation by the SS.

When we reached the Lomboklaan we saw an SS man guarding three bodies. He told us they were terrorists. It seemed such a waste of lives now that the war was over. I was so sad and so indignant that I could not stop myself from asking, 'Why have they been shot? Surely you must know that the war is over?'

'We did it just for fun,' he sneered.

I was horrified and outraged but I could not show it. I had to stay in control of my feelings. I still had a job to do. I was also worried about what would happen to the others who were being held in the front room of De Stroohoed. Through the window I could see my 'cousin' among them. I asked the guard what the SS intended to do with them.

Indicating the hand-grenade he carried attached to his belt, he replied coldly, 'We will make mincemeat out of them.'

It was by now 3 p.m. and the Germans decided to march them to a place near Doorn to execute them. This was going to be wanton murder and a massacre of many innocent people who just happened to be in the wrong place at the wrong time. I managed to exchange a few words with my 'cousin', but he was immediately ordered to walk on.

There was nothing more I could do on the spot, and as I now knew what was going on I walked back to Zonhof with my Czech escort. As soon as he was in his room I dashed across the road to Jan's to report to George. There were so many SS troops about that it did not look feasible to rescue the prisoners, of whom there were thirty.

I felt dreadful. How could the Germans do this? The district nurse, who wanted to give the prisoners some food, was told to join the prisoners. After they had been walking for almost an hour and a half and had almost reached the place of execution, a miracle happened.

Two German cars came along. One of them contained General Blaskowitz, who had just signed the surrender documents on behalf of the German army in the Netherlands. He was on his way back to his headquarters. He stopped his car and asked an officer with him to find out what was going on. When he heard that all these civilians were about to be shot as a reprisal he overruled the decision, since on surrendering only a short time before, he had promised that there would be no more executions. Had such a massacre taken place, he would no doubt have been held responsible. What luck that he had happened to drive along that road at that particular time!

The prisoners, who were very tired and emotionally drained by their experience, trudged silently back towards Leersum. They had only one bicycle, which belonged to the district nurse. She gave it to the Jewish man who had been so badly beaten that, now on the point of collapse, he was incapable of walking all the way back again. He had to be pushed along as he did not have the strength to ride it himself.

All that afternoon the SS continued to search houses and to loot. At Zonhof they took all the English books from the shelves and tore them to pieces. I was unlucky. I had put all my belongings in a suit-case, ready to take them home. The SS took the suitcase and my bicycle, which left me with only the things I stood up in. Fortunately, though, there was nothing incriminating in the case. As I was still wearing my nurse's uniform for safety's sake, I did not have a dress left to wear.

They also called at the house of Adri Bakker. She was hiding a Polish deserter. The Germans asked where her husband was and they also wanted the key to the barn next to her house. She knew weapons were kept there, so she said she did not have the key and she did not know where her husband was either. The Germans threatened to throw a grenade into her house if she did not co-oper-ate. She just shrugged her shoulders and said, 'Go ahead, then.' Luckily it was an idle threat this time and they went away

After the prisoners who had been saved by General Blaskowitz had returned to Leersum, the other forty men who had been kept in the field all day were allowed to go home. They were told to stay indoors for the rest of the day.

Before this happened, however, during the afternoon Ru Selles had heard that some men had been arrested and taken to a field. She also heard that relatives were being allowed to take them overcoats to wear and some food. She thought that her husband, Wim, who had not come home, might be among them, so she went out with a coat for him and some bread. When she left the driveway of her house she saw some bodies lying by the roadside some distance ahead of her. As two Germans were standing there she did not dare to investigate but hurried on. When she did not find Wim in the field with the others she began to worry that he was one of the men whose bodies she had seen earlier.

In the evening, after the Germans had left, Ru asked a neighbour to go and look. He had to return and break the news to her that Wim was indeed one of the victims. Later, two Resistance members of the BS rang her doorbell. They had been on their way to the MOVA meeting that morning, had heard shooting and had remained hidden in the forest all day. Now they asked if they could stay the night at her house. Ru agreed, and in the morning she asked them to help her bring her husband's body home. The three of them carried him on a ladder. She was terribly upset to see that the Germans had even taken his wedding ring. Then Ru walked a mile to Jan Lagemaat's house, leaving her six children, one of whom was a two-month-old baby, alone. Jan arranged for the district nurse to go and help Ru. That day permission was given to take the other bodies to the mortuary and it was decided that they would all be buried with full military honours.

The day before the funeral I went to Ru's with the national flag. I did not know what to say when I saw Ru with the baby in her arms and the other children, all very subdued. Together we draped the flag over the coffin. How does one come to terms with such an unnecessary death? I felt so helpless. When you are young, somehow you do not know how to find the right words – trying to comfort a widow and her children is generally not something you have the experience to cope with at twenty, even if war has brought death that much closer than normal. I found it all deeply distressing.

On the evening of 5 May, and continuing into the night of 6 May, the SS had a great party in Leersum. In addition to their own supplies, they consumed whatever food and alcohol they had been able to loot – some local people had put by a bottle of spirits, with which they had hoped to celebrate the end of the war. One such bottle which did escape the SS had been labelled by a friend of mine with a skull and cross-bones and the formula H_2SO_4 (sulphuric acid).

On the 6th, which was supposed to be our second day of freedom, an SS man called at Mrs Loudon's house to check identity cards. Roelof van Valkenburg was there, as he had used Mrs Loudon's chicken-house as a hiding place the previous night. His papers were in order but the soldier took his Leica camera. The German showed him a pistol, which he said he had taken from a terrorist. Roelof recognised it as one that had belonged to Gilbert Sadi Kirschen (Captain King) and which had been passed on to Jan van Dijk when the agent had returned to Britain. So we now knew that Jan had been captured, though we did not know yet that he had been executed. The SS stayed in Leersum until that afternoon, when they withdrew. We were all thankful to be rid of these bullies and murderers.

On 7 May George and I set out to cycle to Driebergen. I had to borrow a bicycle as mine had been taken, along with my suitcase. Near Doorn we were stopped by two SS men – were they never going to leave us in peace? This time they wanted our bikes. I said I was a nurse and had a permit for mine and he couldn't take it. His answer was to aim his rifle at me and say, 'Choose between giving me your bicycle or being shot.' I had, of course, no choice and I was livid. I had managed to hang on to my bicycle all through the war and now, in the first three days of freedom, I had lost two! It was maddening. Moreover, of course, George and I had to walk another 7 km (4 miles).

The Canadians to the rescue

The Canadians when they did arrive, travelled along the road from Ede to Utrecht and also along the one from Rhenen to Utrecht. The villages that were not on those roads were still very badly off. In Maarn, for example, the SS kept their tanks in the village and they looted all the farms in the neighbourhood. The vicar slipped away and went to the centre of Doorn, where the Canadians were, to ask for help. The SS tanks were withdrawn from Maarn when Allied troops appeared, but these Canadians were artillery men who were not used to dealing with people hiding in forests. The Resistance was hoping for some infantry to come and help to protect the civilians from the marauding SS.

The SS were still in the outskirts of Doorn. In the evening they came out of hiding and terrorised the local people by taking whatever food and civilian clothes they could find and threatening to shoot anyone who resisted them. The situation was so bad that the burgemeester ordered a curfew of his own. If nobody went out after 11 p.m. they could not be shot in the dark streets by the SS. The burgemeester asked the Canadian commander to contact his German counterpart to exert some control over the SS men. This swiftly resulted in the Germans being ordered to surrender and to hand in their weapons. It was not until 4 p.m. on 7 May that the enemy finally left Doorn.

The Canadians had now taken over. It became safer for people to go out. In the afternoon of 9 May, five days into the liberation, Veenendaal was at last freed. People there were also in mourning, because on 7 May three members of the Resistance BS organisation had been shot by the SS. On the night of 8–9 May the Canadians did a sweep of the local forests and captured those SS men who had refused to surrender. No doubt among them were those with very guilty consciences – if they had any – who were now afraid of what might happen to them.

In Doorn the Canadians wanted to pay tribute to Frans van Dijk, the local Resistance leader, who tragically had not lived to see the day of liberation. A Canadian rang the council offices to say that one of their officers would be coming with a wreath. Whoever answered the telephone must have misheard and told the burgemeester that an officer called Reed was coming. When he arrived and was taking tea with the burgemeester's family, the officer asked, 'Why does everybody keep calling me "Captain Reed"? My name is Piper.' Until I did the research for my book and heard this little story, from the daughter of the burgemeester, this officer's name was in the town's archives as 'Captain Reed'.

In Leersum we did not feel like celebrating at first. We still had to hold the funerals of those who had died on Liberation Day. The district commander of the BS came and set up his headquarters in a local hotel. The Resistance occupied one floor and Canadians took over some of the bedrooms. Once the Canadians settled in, however, the local mood changed.

When all the SS men had been removed, we started partying in the evenings as well as during the day. Every few streets there was a party going on. People put up decorations – flags, scraps of material, whatever came to hand – and played music. We danced in the streets and hugged our neighbours. Never mind that we were hungry – our energy came from that deep joy within us that at last, at last, our cares were lifted, the enemy had been defeated and we were free again.

Some people were lucky and were given food by the Canadians. Those boys were generosity itself: they gave everything they had, but there were too many of us lining the streets, waving and shouting as they passed through. Neighbours shared what was going. We could be patient now that we knew help was at hand and we would not have to go without for much longer.

I had been given a tin of corned beef and some biscuits, and I also received some army rations, which I took to my mother. This food tasted better than anything we could remember. Mother had an antique dinner service to which she was very attached. At the beginning of the occupation she had packed it in small crates, which my father had buried, with a few heirlooms, in the garden. Mother's way of celebrating was to have the service dug up straight away and to wash it. Without soap this took some time. There were sixty plates, plus other items. Poor Ank had to dry them all before she could go out and watch the Canadians going past.

We had been dependent on bicycles for transport for so long, and life now changed dramatically. If we wanted to go somewhere we could hold up our hands and a Canadian Jeep or car would stop and take us with them. When my eighty-year-old grandfather heard this from his neighbour's daughter he was impressed. He dearly wanted to visit his daughter, whom he had not seen since the railway strike. He stood beside the main road for two hours, holding up his arm. None of the Canadians stopped. Very disappointed, he returned home. The neighbour's daughter had forgotten to tell him that first he had to change himself into a pretty young girl!

Every evening the Canadians held a dance in Rhenen. A truck would go round all the towns and villages from Driebergen to Rhenen, collecting all the girls who wanted to dance. Naturally I went along too. Strictly at midnight the music for the last dance was played and all the girls left for home. The soldiers were not allowed to accompany us. The Canadian commander was very firm about that.

I had only my nurse's uniform to wear and when a Canadian officer asked me about it and I explained, he gave me one of their uniforms. I still lacked a dress to dance in – the uniform was too warm for that. Having been so cold for so long, it seemed strange to be complaining about the heat! My mother, ever ingenious, ran me up a dress made out of a sheet and her blue checked kitchen curtains. Later I was given coupons for a dress and a coat, but the shops had no stock for some time.

The uniform I had been given was a battledress jacket, trousers, a shirt, black tie and a beret. The trousers were far too long for me and of course they had a front fly. In those days the trousers women wore did up with a zip at the side and no self-respecting girl would be seen wearing men's trousers. What could I do? The local Nazis had been taken into detention in the isolation wing at Valkenheide and among them was a tailor. I took the trousers to him and ordered him to alter them for me, which he did immediately. Our roles had certainly been reversed and I savoured that moment.

It was not all dancing and fun with the Canadians, though. I had a nasty experience early on. An officer came to our headquarters to ask where he could billet his men and pitch some tents. George told him that I knew the area like the back of my hand and that I would go with him and show him.

I took him to a castle on the outskirts of Leersum. They would surely want to house some officers and they had enough farms and fields for the men. The driver remained in the Jeep and I introduced the officer after we had entered the castle. I waited in the hall while he and the owner talked in the study. They took a long time and when they came out I noticed that the drink must have flowed freely as the officer appeared to be a little unsteady on his feet. As I climbed into the Jeep he dismissed his driver, which struck me as odd. I wondered how he was supposed to return to Leersum. The officer then clambered ponderously into the driving seat, drove off very fast in the opposite direction to where our HQ was and went straight down a track off the road, between the woods and a field. He stopped the Jeep suddenly and put his arms round me. I was furious – this was not the way my friends and I had been brought up to behave. In the Resistance we had all been very correct in our relations with each other. Moral standards were strict in those days and there had been no question of doing anything out of place. Besides I was in uniform and we were on official business. Fortunately for me, and unluckily for him, I had had long practice in keeping my wits about me.

'You stupid idiot!' I shouted. 'Look what you are doing!'

'What do you mean?'

'You have driven us straight into a minefield.'

'Where are the mines?'

'I don't know exactly. They are everywhere round here, but the Germans have destroyed the charts. A special unit is coming tomorrow to look for them.'

He turned a very nasty grey colour. 'How are we to get out?' he asked.

'I don't know, but we didn't hit any driving in, so if you can manage to back the Jeep very carefully, driving in exactly the track you made, we might make it.'

This sobered up the officer. He reversed at a snail's pace, returned to the castle, where his driver was waiting patiently – he probably knew what he was like – and told him to drive back.

I complained to George, and from then on if I went on a business trip with a Canadian officer, even if there was a driver, one of our men came too. I thought it was ironic that I had had to fight for the freedom of my country for so long and, having survived that, now I had had to fight off an ally!

I stayed on in the BS and looked after the administration. George had become the CO in our district but did not like the paperwork, so he told me to sign everything on his behalf. One day there was a punch-up in Utrecht between Canadian soldiers and Dutch boys who did not like all the girls going out with Canadians. The town was declared out of bounds to all troops who were not based there.

This caused me a problem because there was a musical with Ginger Rogers and Fred Astaire in the starring roles on at the cinema which I dearly wanted to see. I had heard people talking about it but, never having seen one, I did not know what a musical was. Before the war I had been too young to go to adult films. Three of my friends wanted to come too. We could have gone in civvies, but then we could not have used an army car. Also we would have had to pay for our tickets, whereas entrance was free for anyone in uniform.

Well, you do not lose old skills quickly, so I typed out in my best English on headed BS notepaper an army order, saying that we had to go to the BS headquarters in Utrecht. I stamped it and signed it. I also wrote out a permit for the use of the car.

In the suburbs of Utrecht we were stopped by the Canadian military police. The driver showed the order and we were allowed to go on. It was a marvellous film, which we thoroughly enjoyed. On our return journey the checkpoint was still there but military traffic leaving Utrecht was not stopped. Nobody believed us the next day, but we had had our fun anyway.

Towards the end of the war some leaders of the action groups circulated a warning to their members about the dangers of communism. This was another ideology that might threaten our hard-won freedom. We had to be watchful. As a result, after the war some members joined the Dutch Interior Security Service (the equivalent of the British M.I.5). Among these were Paul Bos and Henny Idenburg. I decided to do the same. It was then the end of 1945 and I did not see myself making a career in the army. I passed all the tests and was given a starting date, but the weekend before I was due to report for work I met a very good friend who questioned my decision. He asked me what I would have done if there had been no war. I said I had always wanted to be a doctor. His comment was, 'So you let Hitler change you plans after all.'

I realised he was right. I found a teacher to help me with the maths and science I had forgotten and needed to brush up, and in 1946 I was accepted to read medicine at Utrecht University. Now I had to learn a different kind of discipline, and methods different from those I had been practising for the last few years, to help save lives.

Epilogue

On 8 May a service of thanksgiving was held in the Dutch Reformed Church in Driebergen. Many of the Jewish people who had been in hiding in the town and surrounding area came to that service. Immediately after the liberation all the Jewish divers had emerged thankfully from their hiding places. There had never been a synagogue in Driebergen, but on 11 May a special service was held for the divers in the same church, and the local minister and the burgemeester – the man who had been sacked by the Germans but had now returned to take up his office again – both made a speech. After that the 120 Jewish survivors separated, as was their custom, with the men on one side of the church and the women on the other, and they held their Friday prayers, followed by Kaddish, the Jewish mourner's prayer for the dead. It must have been the first time in the history of the Netherlands that Kaddish had been said in a Protestant church. It was a very impressive and moving ceremony.

One of the causes of sadness for the Jewish divers during the occupation had been that, if one of them died, he or she could not be given a proper burial. They were usually buried in someone's garden. Claire and Ludwig Hirsch had left some of their furniture and possessions with their neighbours before they went into hiding, and when they returned to collect them they found that two coffins had been added. The neighbour said that she had thought it too awful that a Jewish person might have to be buried in just a sheet. She had not wanted that to happen to her friends the Hirsches. If they were to die, they would at least have a proper coffin. To prepare for the worst she had asked a local carpenter to make two. Now she hoped they would not have to use them for many years to come.

The country was officially free, but nobody knew yet what had happened to the many prisoners who had been sent to the German concentration camps. A time of waiting and hoping began. There had been no news of the prisoners who had been sent from Vught to

Germany on 6 September 1944. The men had been sent to Sachsenhausen. On 20 April this camp was between the Russian and the American front. As the Germans preferred to encounter the Americans and not the Russians, they started evacuating the camp in the direction of the Americans.

The prisoners were sent in groups of 500 and it took two days before they were all marching, without food, through the hail and rain of typical Continental April days. If a prisoner fell and could not immediately get up and go on, he was shot. They started with 36,000 prisoners, 900 of them Dutch. After five days they were all herded into a forest. Only 20,000 had survived so far. Then members of the Swiss Red Cross arrived and they forbade the SS to shoot any more prisoners. The Red Cross brought food and took away the seriously ill.

After walking for another five days, on 4 May the prisoners met, not the Americans, but an advance guard of the British 2nd Army. Only 236 out of the 900 Dutch had won through. Among the survivors was Wim Koumans, who had been imprisoned for sheltering Jewish divers. The Red Cross put him on a plane to Brussels and from there he caught a train. He was astonished to find Arnhem in ruins, but he was able to get a lift home from there, arriving on 10 June. He was received with tears of joy by his family and everyone around. This was a great initial boost to everyone's morale.

The war had taken a great toll. Out of the 107,000 Jews who were deported, only 5,000 returned. The Germans had deported 245 gypsies, and of these only 55 came back. There had been 2,133 executions. In German concentration camps to which 11,000 people had been sent, about 4,000 had died. Many of the 2,500 people who were sent to prisons in Germany did not survive.

As for the Resistance, the BI (Intelligence Bureau) had sent in 43 agents, of whom 17 had lost their lives. The GDN (Dutch Secret Intelligence) lost 27 of its 1,200 members and the LKP (Landelijke Knokploegen) and the LO (Assistance to Divers) together lost 1,671 of their members. Membership of the LKP was about 1,800, and the LO estimated its membership as being between 12,000 and 14,000. The total population at the time was about 9.2 million.

Great economic damage had been done too – for example, to our railways. The Germans had stolen 84 per cent of the locomotives, 98 per cent of the goods wagons and 94 per cent of the passenger coaches. They had also taken 750 km (466 miles) of the 800 km (497 miles) of electrified track, plus much of the other track, and 180 railway bridges had been destroyed.

Soon after the liberation the British M.I.5 opened an office near The Hague to register the names of members of the Resistance. Those who had helped sailors, soldiers and airmen of the British Commonwealth to escape from, or evade capture by, the enemy were given a certificate signed by Air Chief Marshal Tedder, the Deputy Supreme Commander of the Allied Expeditionary Force. Those who had helped Allied soldiers were given a certificate signed by Dwight D. Eisenhower, who had become President of the United States by the time the certificates were sent.

Lord Portal founded the Royal Air Forces Escaping Society. Its members are British or Commonwealth airmen who arrived home safely after having been shot down over enemy or occupied territory. Their helpers (including me) were made honorary members. I was the Netherlands secretary from 1969–86. The society sent us a Christmas card each year until 1994. In May 1994 there was a farewell dinner in London because the society was winding down its activities.

In 1981 a memorial plaque to commemorate the helpers who lost their lives was unveiled in the RAF church, St Clement Danes, in London. The sculptress of the plaque was Elizabeth Lucas Harrison, a granddaughter of Claire and Ludwig Hirsch, who were divers in Driebergen.

The Americans founded the Air Forces Evasion and Escaping Society. They, too, send their helpers an annual Christmas card. In 1988 a plaque was unveiled in the memorial wall in the cemetery of the Air Force Academy in Colorado Springs to honour the memory of the helpers who died while assisting American airmen.

I was one of the many helpers who attended the ceremony at the unveiling of the plaque in London. I was also one of thirty helpers from Belgium, France, Denmark and Yugoslavia, who went to the ceremony at Colorado Springs – we were fewer there because of the distance to travel.

The Israeli government gave the Yad Vashem medal to people who had sheltered a Jewish person. The inscription on the medal is in French. It says: 'Whosoever saves a life saves the whole universe.' These words express one of the basic ideas of the Resistance. My grandfather and aunt both received it, with the right to plant a tree in the Avenue of the Righteous in the Yad Vashem Memorial in Jerusalem. Their citation states: 'As a neighbour was known to work with the Germans their hospitality meant a great risk for their own lives and safety.'

In 1993 at Almere, a new town built on land reclaimed from the sea after the war, the Resistance planted a forest with a tree for every person who had been executed. On the subject of medals, generally speaking, although of course we appreciated the certificates and honorary memberships we were offered, most of the Dutch Resistance did not look for reward. We thought we just did what everyone had a duty to do. Some of the leaders and people who performed what were considered acts of military bravery did receive medals later, but they were few. There was no Resistance medal as there was in France and Belgium. Recently a commemorative medal was invented, like a campaign medal. You had to apply for it yourself, as no official records were made in the Netherlands after the war. I did not apply for one and neither did any of my personal friends. At a rough estimate, about half the people who were entitled to one applied.

Once life had returned to some semblance of order, I took up my studies again and achieved my ambition of qualifying as a doctor. I worked in the Health Service in the UK from 1957 until 1962, after which I returned home and practised as an anaesthetist in Utrecht and later as a medical adviser in The Hague.

Among the others who survived the war, Roelof van Valkenburg became a paediatrician and later the medical superintendent of a hospital. He married Bep Labouchère. He died in 1990. The courier Annie (Ila van den Bosch) married a barrister. Jan Lagemaat played the organ at her wedding service. Annie is now a grandmother and we are still in touch. My friend Ank Prevo started training as a nurse immediately the war was over. A few years after she qualified, she married. George van Spronsen became a sports officer in the Dutch Royal Air Force, reaching the rank of lt-colonel (Dutch Air Force ranks have the same name as army ranks). Several people emigrated: Hein van Remmerden to the USA; Cora and Gerrit de Jong to Canada (where they died some time ago); and Annie Visser to Australia. She remarried there, and has since died. Her son was just a toddler when his father was executed. He told me that his mother used to hide illegal papers and weapons under the mattress in his pram. Jans Lagemaat lived to be eighty-six and her husband, Jan, who was on the village council for many years, died in 1993 at the age of ninety. With seven other members of the Resistance, I was a pallbearer at his funeral. Grandad Pater died in 1960 at the age of eighty-four. His wife, who was three years younger, survived him by another ten years. On 5 May 1995, on the occasion of the fiftieth anniversary of the liberation, a path in the Leersumse Veld was named the Paterpath. The burgemeester invited all surviving members of the Resistance who worked with Grandad to attend the unveiling of the name-plate. Grandad Pater would have liked that.

Some events during the war made such a deep impression that the Dutch commemorate them every year. The February strike is one of these, and the battle of Arnhem is another. With fellow Resisters I attend commemorations during the year, both the national ones and the local ones on anniversaries of the deaths of so many of our friends. Even today, fifty years on, these occasions can be emotional, but they are also good memories of fine men and women of whom we are immensely proud.

Now I am a member of the council that awards pensions to civilian war victims and I am active on committees concerned with keeping in touch with former members of Resistance groups in my part of the country. Most Resistance organisations have a reunion once or twice a year. All the Resistance organisations and those of people who were persecuted and who were in the concentration camps – in all, over twenty groups – are united under one umbrella organisation. This sends Resistance people out to lecture to schools, colleges and other interested groups. We talk about what happened during the war and we warn of the dangers of dictators, discrimination and racism. I know our efforts work. An eleven-year-old recently wrote in an essay: 'Now that that lady has talked to us, I know that I will always have to help people.'

Index of Names